Master Your Own Destiny

The tools and techniques to create your fantastic future

by
Sheila Steptoe

Foreword by
Nick Williams

"A thought-provoking look at how you can harness the power of thought to manifest your destiny."
Randy Gage – Author, Prosperity Mind

authorHOUSE®

AuthorHouse™ UK Ltd.
500 Avebury Boulevard
Central Milton Keynes, MK9 2BE
www.authorhouse.co.uk
Phone: 08001974150

© 2009 Sheila Steptoe. All rights reserved.

No part of this book may be reproduced, stored in a retrieval system, or transmitted by any means without the written permission of the author.

First published by AuthorHouse   5/29/2009

ISBN: 978-1-4389-1493-0 (sc)

Printed in the United States of America
Bloomington, Indiana

This book is printed on acid-free paper.

Cover design and drawings by Geoff Holdsworth

Lots of people pursue personal growth
— when you combine it with *spiritual* growth
you unleash your full potential.
Suddenly, there are no limits any more. . .

What people are saying about this book

Wow, what a thought provoking and stimulating book. I really like the balance between Sheila's actual experiences and guidance for our futures. The fact that the book actually made me stop and think about what I had been doing, was doing and would really like to do in the future was an interesting and soul-searching journey; the exercises helped to put my life and those around me into perspective.

I really liked the spiritual aspect of the book and the gentle introduction of connecting to something greater than our physical beings and exploring - new to me anyway - different theories, in a manner that was not scary but evolutionary. This is a book I will definitely be sharing with others.

— *Caroline Golding*
Nurse Practitioner, Learning Disabilities and Human Givens Therapist

It seems that there is a global spiritual awakening with more and more people looking for spiritual knowledge. Reading *Master Your Own Destiny*, which covers such a wide range of topics, is an excellent starting point. Sheila's writing style reflects her warm compassionate personality, and she imparts knowledge in an easy-to-read way offering examples from her own amazing story. Sheila also suggests simple exercises which are easy to follow and include in our daily lives — but added together are powerful tools for spiritual growth. This book is a must-read for those starting on a spiritual path.

— *Mark Baigent*
Photographer
www.markbaigent.co.uk

Master Your Own Destiny is amongst my top five favourite self help books.

It came just at the right time, when I was making big decisions about my life and my business. Sheila's easy-to-follow simple exercises gave me the tools to question my choices and to realise that which ever direction I take is the right one.

My spiritual awareness has increased and for the first time I know that the journey I am on will take me to my destiny.

— *Margaret Fleming*
Personal and Corporate Image Consultant
www.theimagepractice.co.uk

I wish you lots of success and fun with your book.

— *Gill Edwards*
Author of Living Magically
www.livingmagically.co.uk

After I was made redundant, I didn't know where to turn — so this book could not have come at a better time. I feel as if you're saving me having to read a couple of dozen whole books by other people, and maybe not getting on too well with all of them. By serving me a 'meze' of delicious morsels to try out for credibility and relevance to my own life and belief system first, I suddenly found the answer I was looking for.

In an easy and relaxed style, I loved working through some of the exercises, which have helped me to gain back my confidence and to embrace a new spiritual path as suggested, which has helped me feel whole again.

— *Mandy Tysoe*
Unemployed Personal Assistant

Your words are spoken with love and wisdom. I can feel your truth and love as I read them. Thank you for writing in an easy style which has inspired me.

— *Jackie Dunn*
Evolution Financial Coaching

In the West there is very little spiritual aftercare for those undergoing shifts in consciousness. It was Sheila's insight that was responsible for connecting others to what had happened to me. This began the journey of building a community where people could share their experience, strength and hope with others on the same path. Sheila's integrity and spiritual experience is an asset to us all. God bless you.

— *J C Mac*
Spiritual Lifestyle Coach and Speaker
www.jcmac.net

With wisdom, compassion and empathy, Sheila Steptoe invites you to reconsider your definition of love, fulfilment, wellbeing, and purpose. Reminding each of us that true happiness is a choice, not an accident, *Master Your Own Destiny* offers a personal approach to self-awareness through both joy and adversity. Use it to discover a life that really works for you.

— *Max Eames*
Psychotherapist and author of Under The Hood
www.maxeames.com

Contents

Acknowledgements ix

Foreword.. xi

About me xiii

Introduction xv

Chapter One
My Awakening Begins 1

Chapter Two
Core Conditioning.. 26

Chapter Three
The Power Of Your Mind 54

Chapter Four
Believing In Yourself... 82

Chapter Five
Appreciating life 114

Chapter Six
The Grand Design.. 130

Chapter Seven
Goal setting... 144

Chapter Eight
Spiritual extras.. 161

Chapter Nine
You Can Do This Too.. 190

Appendix A
Ideas For Further Reading 200

Appendix B
Places To Visit Or Read About 205

Appendix C
Further Thinking And Tips 207

Appendix D
Books, People And Websites 211

Appendix E
School For Parents, College For Carers 216

Acknowledgements

There are many times when I say to my friends: 'Thank you for being in my life,' as I acknowledge each one of you as the blessing you are.

Many people inspired me to write this book, and I am grateful to you all and to my work colleagues. I can't mention you all by name but you know who you are!

There are just a few people I have to say a huge thank you to; without you, this book would not be so special to me.

Geoff Holdsworth, a friend and artist, for his patience and lovely drawings … I think I drove you mad!

Mark, Caroline and Margaret, who reviewed my ramblings before I sent them to the editor. Thank you, as you all spurred me on with such wonderful feedback and encouragement.

Max, Nick and Lesley in your own special way.

Everyone who has attended one of my workshops or listened to me giving a talk or presentation, I would also like to thank. Many of you have asked when my next book is coming out, and it has been my pleasure and joy because you've all inspired me as much as I hope I inspired you!

And last but by no means least Fiona Cowan, my editor. I loved that you liked this book from the beginning so I knew I could trust 'my baby' in your hands. You made me cry sometimes with your powerful praise — especially when you said that some of this resonated with you. It's been great fun working together, and your delicate sympathetic tweaking has made this a book I am proud of.

Thank you.

Foreword

You are so much more than you think you are.

We are all wired for joy, happiness and inspiration, because at heart we are spiritual beings. We can't not be, but we can become unaware of who we truly are. Indeed, most of us are asleep to our magnificence. Sometimes it takes a difficult time when we experience pain and suffering to wake us up.

I have met so many people in my life who have waited until the pain gets too bad before they change. They are not being punished, but awakened. When we suffer, the choice each of us faces is this: What will we do with our experience? What meaning will we glean from it?

In essence, we face a decision: Do we build higher defences to keep life out so as to try to save ourselves more pain or do we allow life to awaken us, open us up, dismantle our defences and transform our pain into a gift for ourselves and others?

All over the world we see examples of the former: people wanting revenge to try to feel better, not forgiving so they nurture grievances, but causing more pain and continuing the cycle. Gladly, we are also seeing more examples of the latter. More people than ever want to transform their suffering and end that cycle and awaken.

Sheila is a wonderful living example of taking what life has thrown at her and using it to awaken and transform her challenges, discovering a new foundation for her life. She embodies this ultimate generosity by taking her own experience and offering it as a gift to you. I believe this is one of the most generous things a human being can do. She has woken up to a more powerful existence within her, and is now holding a hand out to you to help you do the same. She has discovered she is more than she thought she was, and now wants to help you discover yourself.

Take her invitation to explore who you truly are, not what you have come to believe you are. You are an amazing being, powerful beyond measure, creative and loving. Enjoy your journey into self-discovery and enjoy having Sheila be one of your guides into the true you.

Nick Williams, London, 2009

About me

When I was a child I saw my life as just plain fun. Nothing fazed me.

Then I grew up and this big wide world came calling. Hmmm… *life is not always such fun*, I soon realised! But, through the eyes of a child, you can do anything you want. The magic of life can be wondrous if you choose to open your eyes — or you can walk around in darkness.

Over time, many things happened in my life. However, the last fifteen years have been a real adventure. I have gone from being an ordinary housewife with a little part-time job to having a career which a few years ago I had never imagined. I have gone with my flow and I have had support from many unexpected sources!

A few years ago I wrote a book which some of you will have read. I had an urge to write another — but, like many people, procrastinated for some time until the urge became so strong I couldn't resist any longer. So many brilliant things had happened to me that I wanted to share them and give hope to other people. A few of these stories I have touched upon again in this book, because they are so profound. As you read on, you will see how these events have changed my life.

I want to give *you* a glimpse of what life could be like, if you suddenly decided to take a leap of faith and get more meaning into your life, and go for what you truly desire.

We all have down times. Outside influences can have an enormous effect on us as human beings, especially in this economic crisis. However, we need not feel it all has to be doom and gloom; life is meant to be fulfilling and wonderful. It can and should be.

Over the years, my fun journey has led me to do lots of things I probably shouldn't, such as indulge in red wine or something a little stronger to relax occasionally. But my biggest love is socialising! I love people, discussions till late at night, and trying to put the world to rights in a friend's house having dinner round the table.

I have become a daredevil too. I have gone deep-sea diving, ridden on horseback in the Australian outback, driven around a race track, tried paint-balling, go-karting and even White Water Rafting in Australia — which was the most hell raising experience. And I am going to do something else too … but you will have to read to the end of the book to find out what that is. Don't peek yet as you will spoil the fun!

Over the years I have trained as a Counsellor, Life Coach and now I am studying Quantum Physics because it fascinates me. I have worked for some of the top-selling national newspapers as an advertising sales representative, a job I loved but which never fulfilled me.

Life moves on if you go with your flow, and I have now found a career which I adore; I can never see myself retiring. My next mission is to travel the world and to be able to visit and see many different cultures and places. I might even spend three months in South America and volunteer to help in an orphanage and then travel … although I need to get fit first!

I love my little cottage, my friends and family, reading and learning new things. But I also value peace and quiet by spending time on my own or walking in nature. Many people have helped me on my journey where we have laughed or cried together and I am eternally grateful to everyone. Thank you for being in my life.

With love, light, blessings and smiles,

Sheila

Introduction

Something drew you to this book. The reason why you picked it up may be connected with the reason why I wrote it. Let's see if some of this resonates with you:

Are you aware that your life so far is only part of a bigger picture? Are you curious about where it will lead you next, and in the longer term? Do you wonder how much choice you have in the directions your life takes?

Do you feel ready to come with me on a colourful, eventful journey? Are you ready to ignite something deep inside that you can't touch, smell or even taste? Do you want to grow into a person who is able to create more passion, giving your life more depth and meaning?

Are you ready to open your heart to your life? If you are, this book will be the start of an amazing journey. All you have to do is let it happen. Find that gift that everyone has within themselves; don't let it remain hidden any longer.

You may be wondering why on earth you should pick up a book that says, *Master your own destiny*, let alone read it. Don't worry, that just means you are normal! Remember: nobody else can do it for you.

There are many who would suggest that believing in something incredible for your life is just a fantasy, a daydream, and that you should stick to reality.

Many people believe that if they read an inspiring book or hear a motivational speaker; suddenly magical things are going to happen. Just like that. You have every intention of taking action on the things you've learned and that have inspired you — but you'll do it next week or after you've done something else first!.

Have you noticed we are in a time of great change? People are seeking out a deeper sense of connection, and acknowledging parts of themselves that they have repressed for years. Many people feel empty inside; they have reached a turning-point and wish to fill that void.

You may have reached a crossroads in life, or begun to question new events that may have started to happen. Which direction should you take, when you have never really challenged yourself before, and just drifted through life as many people do? You may be scared and confused about what might happen if you fail. Fear, procrastination or self-doubt keep limiting your beliefs.

If you can relate to any of the above please be assured that, if you read on, you will find something different in these pages.

Like you, I have read many books, attended courses, listened to great speakers. Some of them have been marvellous, some mind-blowing and others a load of old waffle. Don't get me wrong: I have always come away with or read something I could act upon. But some don't get to the point quickly enough. Or they repeat things too often and use superficial words. The hype can override the golden nuggets I want to discover, buried deep inside.

Some talk about what *you* should be doing, simply because that is what *they* are doing. They make it sound so easy — but they never seem to mention that, sometimes, the time is not right for you to embrace all this wonderful stuff.

There are many reasons why you may not take action, even though the message inspires you:

- There is too much to think about. So many different ideas are bandied about: who is right and who is wrong?
- Your own life journey is individual and highly personal. So is your spiritual journey. It can not be organised or regulated. It is untrue that everyone should follow one 'true' path. Listen to your *own* truth.
- You may not feel comfortable with what people are telling you, or fully understand what they truly mean.
- You may have reached a crossroads after something devastating happened. You want to emerge as a new confident person but are not sure how to do that.
- You have started on a spiritual journey and want to learn more but at your own pace.
- You want your own *Aha!* moment to happen but it all doesn't make sense yet, so you are still searching.
- Your life may feel comfortable as it is, and you don't want to 'rock the boat'.
- You may not believe that something wonderful can happen to you. Other people are just *lucky*.

It isn't always easy but it can be done. Those experts are right in a way. It's just a matter of timing, being ready and finding what resonates with you.

People will *tell* you what you should or should not be doing, and that's all very well — but they aren't you. We are all different; what works for some doesn't work for all. No-one else can solve your problems, help you achieve what you want, or resolve your issues. But if you truly want to, *you* can work for *you*. You can create your own success, as I have done, in your own unique way.

My aim is to share my story with you as an example, combined with some of the knowledge and lessons I have learned. I have arrived at many crossroads in my life, as you will see. I used to feel like a butterfly trapped in a cage, and then the door was opened. I want to open that door for you, so you feel truly alive. Remember those reasons or excuses why you keep putting things off? By the end of this book I hope that some of those will disappear and the door of your cage will have flown wide open!

I will introduce you to some new concepts that I have experienced over the last fifteen years. Combining spiritual growth with personal growth sets you free from limits.

How does this journey begin?

The first thing to discover is how to open your mind to your own inner power and to the universal energy surrounding you. Powerful sources of wisdom can kick-start changes which will give you amazing results, both personally and professionally — but only if you understand how to recognise and harness them.

Is there something out there, a force, a factor, a power infinitely more powerful than you can imagine? Well, yes, there is. This power is connected to your conscious and subconscious mind and to your soul — your *Higher Self*. You choose to be born for a reason; there is something you have to discover in this lifetime. Tapping into this power can help you awaken to the person you are so you can begin to feel more serene and complete.

Many people are talking about this power now, and I have experienced it in some remarkable ways which I want to share with you. This is what I call help from the Universe and our 'unseen friends'.

I may nudge you outside your comfort zone occasionally — but when you have taken that leap of faith, you will feel amazing. You'll be saying: 'Done that — what's next?' instead of: 'One day I'm going to…' or: 'If only…'

Once you start it is very difficult to stop. So many new doors will open that you'll be wondering why you left it so long to get started.

A whole new world is waiting for you; a world that is exciting, fun and will give your life more meaning and fulfilment. That is what your life should be about, and it's what we all deserve but don't always get. We are all unique with our own special gifts and talents — but you need to find the love and joy that resonates inside, to enable you to walk your own special path.

Have you ever asked yourself any of these questions?
- How can I gain greater meaning to my life?
- What is life all about? Is this all there is?
- Why am I here and what is my purpose?
- Who am I? (Your name may be 'xxxx' but who is the person inside you?)
- What is missing?

As I tell you my own story you will see that everyone's life has a blueprint; something of which, until a few years ago, I was completely unaware. I just thought you got on with life and never questioned anything, and I think that is how most people live. I had no idea that certain things happened to me for a reason, both good and bad. At the time I didn't question why certain events had occurred. It's only on looking back that I have realised the reason behind each experience. Now, I learn from them and realise that some are my lessons I have come here to learn in this School of the Universe. Even if you remember reading about these experiences before….I have the benefit of greater hindsight now, and have taken far deeper meanings from them than I could at the time they were happening to me.

I hope by the end of this book that you will begin to understand a bit more about how life and the Universe can work together.

Life is a journey to be enjoyed, not endured. I want you to discover your life's blueprint, and be happier and achieve your goals just as I have done. I want you to experience your own *Aha!* moment, which could be only a few pages away.

Why this book is different

This book comes straight to the point. It's easy to understand and there are many nuggets right there on the surface; you can just pick them up without having to dig. It also has many reference points, so you can take a particular subject of interest further if you want to. I want to whet your appetite for exploration.

This is your book more than mine, and I want you to work at it at a pace that suits you. That may be gently and slowly, or you can take a huge leap of faith if you prefer; this is your valuable time, your opportunity and you will explore your own experiences, achievements and joy.

Before we start, here are a few tips which should make this easier for you:

- Have you noticed that the title does not include the words 'How to'? That's because the 'how to' bit is up to you.
- You may decide to read the whole book in one go. If you do, don't be afraid to make pencil marks against those things that catch your attention and that you feel you need to work on. Make quick notes if you want to.
- I suggest that it's best to digest each section separately *before* you move on to the next section. Work through some of the ideas and issues which come up. This might be over a couple of hours, a couple of days or even a couple of months.
- You may have some wonderful *Aha!* moments and inspirations, which you will want or need to think about and write down. The *how, why, when,* etc will also come to you, and some of these cannot be rushed. Remember that there are *no right or*

wrong answers, and that your thoughts will change, modify or expand as you read further on.
- Occasionally you may find that a painful memory will emerge. The beautiful thing, about recognising this and releasing it, is that it creates the space for magical things to flow into your life that are more fully aligned with the person that you are becoming or want to be. Sometimes you need to go back to a core issue, because things can be buried deep in your subconscious minds for years — and often these are your fears and our stumbling blocks. Once they have been addressed, it lifts a huge weight off your shoulders.
- I show you different ways and ideas, remind you of some simple things and give you hints, tips and suggestions. However, nothing will change in your life, nothing will grow in your life *unless you make it happen*.
- You don't need to understand this entire book the first time you read it. It is more important that you learn the *process*. As you read on, a shift will take place within you. Your inner light will shine through when you're ready.
- You may need to read some of the chapters a couple of times to digest all the golden nuggets.
- *The choice is yours*. Your commitment to yourself is what produces results. It is about valuing every part of yourself. You can work through this book with imagination, purpose and a sense of fun and achieve what you want, or you can work through it in a half-hearted fashion. The results you get will reflect the effort you put in!
- This book will take you on a journey from your childhood to where you are now so that you can *move on from the past*, *live in the now* and *look to the future*.

Among other things, you will…
- Learn to have unconditional acceptance of yourself — just as you are — and you will grow in confidence.
- Start to have a personal relationship with yourself, and to find your own happiness.
- Develop a sense of inner knowing and serenity.

- Acquire skills and knowledge that will last a lifetime.
- Have fabulous ideas, and find the inspiration to reach your goals, so that you can start changing your life straight away.
- Learn to use the universal energy surrounding you, helping you to understand how life works in a simple format. This may encourage you to look further into different areas which interest you.
- Learn that you are not alone and that you can have more fun, excitement and meaning in your life.
- Bring out the gifts you have, so that you can walk the true path of your calling in life.
- Consider throwing away your text books, stop being guided solely by your brain, and start living from the infinite wisdom of your heart.
- Reach the deep truth within you.

You may find it helpful to discuss some of the subjects in this book with others. Talk to like-minded people, friends, family or professionals about the things you feel, the wonderful ideas you get, or issues which may come up or that you don't understand. This will help you to create the success you really deserve.

I hope this book will help you love yourself and your life so that you live in joy.

Enjoy your read.

Chapter One

My Awakening Begins

Once upon a time, a little while ago, I discovered a truth so exquisitely beautiful that, when I connected to it, my life could never be the same again. I had found the infinite wisdom within my own heart and soul.

Before then I had been happily drifting along, accepting and doing the best I could as I had no idea what my understanding of the meaning of a more powerful existence might be like. I never questioned anything … until one day I realised with a shock that I felt like a butterfly trapped in a cage.

To be able to fly freely and to follow my heart had always been my dream — but until recently I didn't know how. Then the door was opened, and now I feel as though I can achieve anything I want to.

In the few years since that happened, my life has soared beyond my wildest dreams, and is still doing so. I keep pinching myself, hardly able to believe how everything has changed and how much I am learning from this wonderful experience called Life.

I'd always thought that a rollercoaster was just a fairground ride. Suddenly I realised that my life, from birth until recently, had been spent as a passenger in one of those carriages! You might say that life sometimes has a funny sense of humour — and it's not always amusing!

At other times the wonders of this world and the Universe continue to amaze me.

Many times in my life I have been at a crossroads, and often I could have gone under. However, I have always had a positive attitude and a strong belief in myself, so I haven't spent my life saying: *If only…*

I've had my share of life's challenges, including twice being expelled and a drop-out at school, surviving skin cancer for more than 23 years, experiencing the devastation when my husband suddenly walked out after 21 years of a very happy marriage, and being even more heartbroken when my own daughter stopped me from seeing my granddaughter for more than three years.

In addition I have been through bereavement and unemployment, and surprisingly I have found a strength deep inside which allowed me to grow through each experience. There is light at the end of the tunnel and I have now come to a stage where I feel truly alive to my own purpose and to really love being 'me'. I now have true freedom.

It's hard to describe how wonderful this feels. I want *you* to start experiencing this, and to have a 'knowing' deep inside that you too can reach serenity.

Serenity is a place which allows you to believe in your self and your life's purpose; the struggles of life gradually start drifting away. This has given me so much more than I ever realised I could have. I never thought a few years ago, at the tender age of 55, that I would write a book — let alone two! Nor that I would completely change my career, to something that has opened up a new world for me.

I loved my job as a Health Care Adviser with BUPA — but I have now chosen to walk a completely different path which certainly meant stepping outside my comfort zone. However it is more aligned with the authentic person I am becoming. Today, I give motivational and spiritual talks to large audiences and smaller groups of people, in the public sector as well as the business sector, and run my own workshops in addition to coaching private individuals.

This sensational journey has put me on primetime television and radio, led me into the Professional Speakers Association, given me the opportunity to write as a columnist for magazines, and more. This is not just theory, it's all come from things I have practised, experienced or used in my own life.

I'm an ordinary person, just like you. I have done nothing that you could not do yourself. I haven't sailed around the world, run the London Marathon or climbed Mount Everest! The only way I may differ from you is that I have been lucky enough to have learned and understood how to embrace spirituality, which went on to teach me so much, and to have welcomed some new 'unseen friends' into my life.

No, I am *not* one of those wacky new age revellers who believe they have to chant continuously on the top of a mountain or wear odd baggy clothes and no shoes. I am an ordinary fun-loving twenty-first century person just like you… but inside that person, I have learned to reach my true self and my inner soul.

I know that I have been guided by some force bigger and higher than myself. It has helped me to believe in myself and, without doubt, this has given me the confidence and support to take chances and step far outside my comfort zone. I have experienced that *'wow'* factor so many times that I know I am following my life's blueprint, which the Universe had planned for me in the very beginning. I now have a life and a business which fills me with pride, passion, purpose and fun.

It is one thing to connect with the path of true calling — and another thing entirely to have the courage to walk that path.

SOMETHING TO THINK ABOUT

Ask yourself whether you have ever had a powerful 'inner knowing' about any of these sensations:

- You knew you were going in the right direction. Or the wrong direction. *How did that feel?*

- You felt as if you were swimming against the tide of your life. *How do you think you would feel if life were effortless rather than a struggle?*

- You were confident that you had achieved as much as you could reasonably expect to, at that stage in your life. Or you were frustrated by how little you had to show for your life so far. *Do you still feel contented or frustrated? Do you want to achieve your goals in an inspired and meaningful way? If so, please read on.*

- You realised that emotional pain can be a gift, as long as you could keep your faith and learn from it. *Do you look back now and see the gift it brought you? Does the memory of the pain still taint the beauty of the gift?*

- You understood that success means different things to different people; it can mean finding your heart and soul so you have the courage, the determination and the will to become the person you believe you were meant to be. *Or do you still define success in terms of having things, as most people do? Have you started to shift your definition of it?*

- You realised that who you are at this moment is just fine —

you just need to learn how to shine. *Are you comfortable in your own skin and spirit?*

- You understood that everybody is unique and gifted, with something important to offer the world or to others. *Do you look for what is special, even about people who may seem challenging or difficult? Can you imagine seeing everyone that way?*

Visualise that person; feel how you would feel, being that person, and bring the emotion of that feeling to the surface. Until now you may have only dreamt of a life beyond the constrictions placed upon you by outside influences — but you can be the authentic person you were meant to be.

Start by setting yourself one or two realistic goals — but they must have a purpose or you won't reach them. When you own your personal goals, that is when you start to reach them.

It wasn't always like this

Fifteen years ago, the Universe threw something at me that I wasn't expecting. Abruptly, my life crashed.

In hindsight, I'm glad that the Universe decided I needed a kick up the backside. At the time, however, I was completely derailed.

It might sound like a cliché — however, I wish I had known back then what I know now! It would have helped me to understand what was suddenly going on. It might have helped me to see more quickly how this life experience that we each have really *works*.

We do start out with a life plan but, after we're born, we gradually forget it. Your subconscious mind does remember and you agree to come on this journey. Think of it as a School of the Universe and part of a much bigger picture.

It is often said that we all come into this world for a reason and a purpose. Some people come to learn lessons, some to teach, and some to fulfil a particular task, but we are each born with the skills we will need for our individual life's purpose.

There is something that you have to discover in this lifetime, and that's why you are here. You may already know your *reason* — but your *purpose* could still be hidden. It may be that the reason you forget your life plan is because, if you knew what lay ahead, you might not want to go on. On the other hand, if we didn't experience the bad as well as the good, how would we know the difference and be able to appreciate the joys of the world?

If you're interested in how I found some of the answers which have helped me follow my life's blueprint, and what I now know is the bigger picture — the grand plan the Universe had for me — stay with me through this book and share my journey. Even if you recognise some of the events that happened to me, you may be surprised by what I have learned from them.

How it began for me

I was living a 'normal' life. I was happy, married with two wonderful children, and working part-time as a sales rep on my local newspaper. I had no inkling that my life was about to change in some of the most devastating ways possible — but also in the most beautiful of ways too. I was plunged into a deep dark hole but eventually I came out again with a shining light.

One summer evening, my husband suddenly walked out of what we had both thought was a very happy marriage of 21 years. He was having a mid-life crisis and had found someone else.

Our children and I were instantly overwhelmed with shock.

A few months prior to this devastation, both my Father and Mother-in-law had died, and my Mum was to die only a year later. My Father-in-law also suffered a stroke. Clearly, it was not the best time in my life. Having said that, because I was at such a low point, my whole life was about to open up and evolve into something I never imagined possible; it was the start of an amazing spiritual journey.

I had never thought about anything *spiritual* before; I didn't need to. I had no real religion or other belief system, or even any views on the subject. It was of no particular interest to me or to my friends. You may have heard of people who have discovered religion in the middle of a crisis and that it can be a turning point. Some will say that it is something to cling to — and I agree that maybe it is.

But this experience, to me, had nothing to do with religion. This was different: it was a gentle awakening to something extremely powerful for which as yet I had no name.

Whatever belief system you have right now — whether you believe in God/Mohammad/ Buddha/Source — it makes no difference to what I am talking about. *Religion* has nothing to do with being *spiritual*; we are all *one*. Old 'spirituality' is religion; the new spirituality means recognising the feeling of being alive, with a shift in consciousness to awaken yourself. The new spirituality gives you a freedom beyond measure.

There is a lovely saying from the book *Conversations with God* written by Neale Donald Walsch: 'Ours is not a better way. Ours is merely another way. Who is to say whose way is right or wrong?' This can be said for all religions. Spirituality is about believing in yourself and getting the most from life. It's about being grounded as the authentic you, and being able to live your life's purpose with comfort and ease.

- What have you done at times of great trouble, anguish, grief or stress?
- Did you find yourself unexpectedly praying? Who did you pray to and did it give you comfort? Perhaps you thought that would be silly so you talked to other people instead, or did you find yourself struggling alone?
- How has it helped? What worked, and what didn't work?
- Do you believe that religion and spirituality are the same thing? Because if you do, please read on!

My turning point

Humans say: 'I will believe it when I see it.'
Angels say: 'You will see it when you believe it.'
— Anonymous

Before all this happened, my life had been just fine. I'd had a great childhood, travelled in my teenage years and generally enjoyed life to the full.

I settled down and got married in my mid-twenties. We bought a rundown 400-year-old cottage which needed renovation. We then renovated a Grade II Listed Victorian property which became the family home. My husband ran a successful business, we were happy and we had a great social circle. The kids were doing well and growing up quickly. Life was good; it had ups and downs but I had always coped with the downs before, even when I contracted cancer.

So, to find myself all of a sudden sinking into a deep dark hole was awful. That was such a lonely place. It was all such a shock that I wasn't able to function as I'd used to, because I was becoming emotionally drained. Emotional stress can be far harder to deal with than physical pain.

My way of coping was talking to friends and I am so thankful to all of them and my children for helping me get through. But they couldn't feel or take away my pain or the loss I felt. When you lose a parent, you need time to grieve … and then suddenly my husband leaving was even worse, far more painful. I so desperately wanted a cuddle and a closeness which you can only feel with a partner — and that is exactly what was missing.

Over time, the days gradually became easier to fill than the night times or weekends, which tend to be family times. I felt empty, and kept myself busy going to work in the beginning — but through circumstances which you will read about later that too came to an end.

During the next few months I had many ups and downs. Good times began to happen now and then, and next I would suddenly crash and be back at square one. Some music or a person talking would bring it all flooding back.

The worst time was as winter was drawing in, and my husband was starting to take his new lover out to social functions. Somehow this made it become *real*. I couldn't hide from it any more. In my mind, she had been in the background and I could block her out — because I'd never wanted to confront her. My children did but not I, for some reason.

Then one dark cold miserable evening, when Bob and his new partner were going to a special function where it should have been me on his arm, I became hysterical as the loneliness really hit me. A friend Lesley Elliott came over to sit with me. We had been chatting for about an hour when suddenly, out of nowhere, I had a most beautiful sensation which I could not explain: I went all shivery, with a delicious tingle that gently passed over my entire body. I hadn't created this, so how could I feel it?

Lesley casually remarked: 'Your guides and Angels are in the room. They've come to reassure you that you're not alone. You are feeling them touching you. They're just here to keep you company. Don't worry, everything will be fine.'

What was she talking about? I had no idea.

At the age of 15 I once visited a clairvoyant at the end of a pier just for fun, and then forgot about it. Many of us do something like that as kids. However, for some reason since Bob left I had been finding myself drawn to the idea that perhaps there was someone out there who could give me some kind of answer … and I had no idea why.

So, I asked myself whether mystic people are all necessarily quite as strange and wacky as they had been made out to be on the television. Do they all wear purple, and do they all look into crystal balls as the lady at the end of the pier did? I wasn't quite sure what to expect. How could a set of Tarot cards give those people the answers I was looking for?

I wanted them to tell me that my husband was coming back and that I would be all right. Some of these people were rather odd, sitting in their little dark tents — but most of them were so beautiful that I was stunned. They were kind, gentle, non-judgemental. They simply gave me the information they received. I couldn't always relate to what they told me, some of them gave me amazing information, and others told me things I did not want to hear.

At one exhibition I attended, I remember visiting two different clairvoyants on the same day because I didn't like what the first lady told me!

I had no idea how these people worked or where they got their information — and it didn't seem to matter because at the time it was very comforting. Of course, they couldn't give me *answers* because these have to come from within. However, they did help me realise that there might be a spiritual dimension to finding answers I was looking for.

Just a few months later, my Mum died and I went to pieces. Three losses in less than three years were too much. Had my husband still been around, I might have coped better with the loss of my parents, but instead I felt very alone.

What I did not appreciate was that this was the start of my beautiful journey, a journey which has transformed my life.

Without realising it, I was teaching myself meditation. I had learned how to do it years before in Yoga classes but hadn't practised. It was mostly when I was upset and crying and really needed to chill out that I started to shut out my thoughts. I was still experiencing the beautiful tingling, which was getting much stronger, and now I suddenly started seeing beautiful colours before my eyes when I closed them. The colours just swirled around and around in front of me, gorgeous to watch. When you shut your eyes you normally just see black, yet I was seeing various shades of the colour blue, several pinks and a vivid indigo. At other times I would see greens, reds or yellows, always combined with white.

Then I started to hear, very gently, classical music in my right ear — never my left. How could this be? If you hear music from the radio you hear it in both ears, yet this was definitely only in only one. I never questioned it, being so peaceful, even though I don't particularly enjoy classical music.

All this was beginning to intrigue me. The music, the colours, the tingles — where were they coming from? I couldn't talk in depth to anyone. Some of my friends felt that I had lost the plot (some still do). So, I took myself to a bookshop, where *Opening to Channel: How to Connect with your Guide,* by Sanaya Roman and Duane Packer, jumped out at me. Once I started reading, I couldn't put it down.

Slowly but surely, I began to accept that there must be someone or something out there. There was no way *I* could have created all those tingles, the wave of colours and the beautiful music. So, who was my guide and where was he or she?

In the book, it suggests that you take things slowly, and think seriously about opening up to 'channel', because amazing things will begin to happen.

Suddenly, different events occurred which were difficult to explain. I wasn't looking for romance but I met Graham when our eyes met across a crowded room and we started a beautiful relationship. However, I wasn't strong so I spent many hours waiting by the phone — just like Bridget Jones in the film! But suddenly I kept bumping into him in the most extraordinary places. His car would pull up next to mine in a traffic queue on the motorway … when I hadn't seen him for weeks. Then in another traffic jam on a smaller road he would be going one way while I was going the other and our cars ended up side by side!

The first time it happened I nearly crashed my car, so surprised to see him driving along the same road, miles from home. Over the course of the next two years, something like this would happen more than 40 times. I lost count in the end.

They say there is no such thing as a coincidence. Later, I learned that I was putting my thoughts about seeing him out into the Universe, and 'they' had arranged for me to see him. Nearly every incident prompted him to call, and he would come back into my life for a while, or we would just chat side by side in the car. Amazing. (There are more explanations in Chapter Three.)

This sort of event is called Synchronicity. Psychologist Carl Jung theorised that synchronicities occur when universal forces are aligned with the experiences of an individual, leading to coincidences that appear to be more than just chance. These incidents happen because everything in the Universe is innately connected.

Jung believed that such events can be called forth by an individual's unconscious needs. Nothing occurs randomly. Rather, we draw certain people, situations, and blessings to ourselves and that synchronicity is the phenomenon of meaningful coincidence. It is a resemblance, correspondence, or connection between something going on outside us and something happening inside us. Synchronicity is the surprise that something suddenly fits!

These events are connections that guide us, warn us, or confirm us on our path to our destiny. It can appear as one striking event that sets off a chain reaction. It is always unexpected and somehow uncanny in its accuracy of connection or revelation. This is what makes it impossible to dismiss synchronicity as mere coincidence. It is a word made from two Greek terms meaning 'joined with' and 'time'.

You can read more about this in David Richo's fabulous book *Unexpected Miracles: The Gift of Synchronicity and How to Open It*. I read somewhere else that synchronicity is when God winks at you … what a lovely thought!

SOMETHING TO THINK ABOUT

At some time in our lives each of us has experienced synchronicity. Yet, how many times have you missed the opportunities it presents? Or were you so grateful that you burst out laughing at the beauty of it? These events are more than just the little coincidences of life.

- Think back to when something very unexpected happened. What were you looking for just then? Did it bring an unexpected pleasure or the answer you were seeking?
- You will probably find that it has happened on more than one occasion. Remember the other times, too.
- Did you suddenly find yourself in the right place at the right time? Did you bump into someone you had been thinking about? Were you suddenly introduced to a person who could help you in some way, perhaps in business?
- Was it just when you thought you were on the brink of something, perhaps devastating, that your saviour suddenly appeared?

This happened to a very good friend of mine recently. Becky's boyfriend had starting telling her that she was not beautiful and she was distraught. Apparently, in his eyes, she needed a nose reconstruction and to lose weight — because he wanted a 'perfect' model on his arm and she did not fit the bill. Did this man think he was perfect himself? Becky is one of the most beautiful people you could meet. All she wanted, after she had quite rightly thrown him out, was a cuddle.

Later that night, lying in her bed, snuggled under her duvet with red eyes and tears streaming down her face, she heard a knock at her door. It was dark, wet and it was midnight. What should she do? She was alone in her flat but somehow she knew it would be safe to open the door.

Standing on her doorstep was her first-ever boyfriend. He said: 'I've been thinking about you and want to give you a cuddle.' Becky hadn't spoken to him in months but somehow he *just knew*.

He couldn't keep that feeling to himself because it was so strong and powerful that he just had to visit her. Of course at the time he had no idea why!

I have since asked Becky whether this re-kindled their relationship. Unfortunately not; they do have a special friendship now, as they had both moved on emotionally, but the spiritual bond will always be there.

It gets even better

I began to see pictures when my eyes were closed, and also when they were open. It was like having my own cinema screen right in front of me, as some of them were like mini films. I still remember vividly the very first picture I saw, like a coloured postage stamp, which was of a lady in the Moll Flanders era wearing a white frilly bonnet, looking down at me. It was as clear as clear could be. I have no idea who this lady was — but the experience and the picture were so beautiful that I never questioned it.

Then I started seeing moving pictures on the wooden beams in my cottage. To give you an example, one day Graham was due to come over, and he was late. I found myself meditating and 'they' showed me a moving picture of him with a few friends playing squash. He turned up four hours later and I asked him where he had been. Guess what — he had been playing squash and, sorry, the game had run on longer than expected!

How these pictures were 'beamed' down to me at the time I had no idea. I saw many of them in all sorts of places and it fascinated me. I remember seeing, early one morning on my bedroom ceiling, a double-page spread of a newspaper article. Lo and behold, when I ventured down to the kitchen to get my morning coffee, on opening the paper there was the exact same article!

It also came as a huge surprise to learn that at night I wasn't always completely alone in my bedroom! I would be fast asleep and then suddenly at about four in the morning I'd hear a man's voice gently speaking to me, again only in my right ear. Many times I would wake up thinking someone was in my room — only to find myself alone.

Often he would gently say my name, at other times he would give me a message. Always, he spoke in a lovely gentle tone. I began to call him *Bluey* — because I didn't know his name but he always appeared when I was seeing the colour blue.

Something wonderful was happening to me and I wanted to learn more. I was also beginning to see that the Universe works in mysterious ways, and that the bigger picture of our lives is never revealed as we think. It's only when you look back that you can see why some things happen. It is called destiny or fate.

A change of management at the local newspaper where I worked was making me unhappy and I decided to leave my job. I also had to sell the family home and down-size to a smaller cottage. And then my eye was caught by an advertisement in one of the Sunday papers advertising cheap flights to Australia over Christmas. I had been to Australia twice before, once as a family and then I took another trip to see my sister Maryanne in Perth just after my husband left — but this time I had no idea why I was going.

My son was going anyway, as my brother-in-law had just offered him a job in Perth. So I booked two tickets for my daughter and myself, not realising that there was a significant reason for my trip.

We were staying with my sister when, in the very early hours of Christmas Day morning, we got a call from Liz, one of our sisters in the UK, to say that Mum had died suddenly from a stroke. This came as an enormous shock. She had been healthy and spending the Christmas break in London with Liz and her family.

Maryanne had always felt a little guilty about emigrating, because our parents were elderly when she left. She had always said that she dreaded the day anything happened to them and she would be on her own on the other side of the world. Well, of course, she wasn't on her own — I had been sent there to be with her. *That* was the reason for my trip.

I was beginning to learn that if you are open and relaxed about our life, it can be a wonderful journey. Dreadful things happen and beautiful things happen, too. I became more consciously aware of this when I was at college doing a Counselling degree. In one of my tutorials, I had been asked to 'draw my life'. Being no artist, I wondered why on earth I should — and what it might reveal.

I found myself drawing a river. On the banks of the river were the big events in my life. Each time something major had happened I had clung to the side … and then I was gently brought back to the river and where I was meant to be. I could see the beginning of the ocean and I was nearly there. You will have heard of the expression 'going with the flow' — and that is exactly what I was doing.

It uplifted me to realise that in some ways my life had been mapped out for me, that everything would be all right, but that we all have 'free will' and can still make choices. Sometimes you make choices that are good for your growth, and at other times you may take a wrong turning. However, I believe that you are always brought back to where you are meant to be.

You can struggle against it. Your ego can tell you that it knows best, and you can be stubborn, yet you have a reason to be here on this Earth. Sometimes you have lessons to learn that may not be to your liking — but you can move on to better things.

Going with the flow doesn't mean giving up control of your sense of direction; nothing could be further from the truth. *Going with the flow* means feeling that everything in your life is going in the right direction, you are happy, and everything becomes effortless. This happens when you begin to trust yourself and doors begin to open that you never imagined were possible.

You become a magnet, and events like synchronicity begin to happen more often.

Drawing your own life

> This can reveal many things and you may find a pattern running through your life.
> - Put an emotion next to something that has happened.
> - Include people who may have had a big influence in your life.
> - Colour it if you want to, or cut out pictures from a magazine if you would prefer.
> - Look at some of the lessons you have learned — what have they taught you?
> - Put your big achievements in there, too.
> - Be proud — and be ready for some powerful emotional responses.

Some of my colleagues drew trees with each leaf being a different event. There are no rules. Draw your life the way you feel you want to.

This exercise should help you focus on the patterns in your life: positive and negative relationships, good experiences and the bad ones. It should help you to see how you would like to move forward.

When you have finished, question yourself. How do you feel? Is there a pattern or is each experience different? What has life taught you? How can you change it, if it needs changing? Are you going with your flow and being the authentic you?

Thoughts are like radio signals

I have learned that we are constantly manifesting things in our lives, whether or not we are conscious of it. This includes negative things as well as positive. Once I understood that every thought I have is like a radio signal going out to the Universe, where someone is listening and then my wishes are granted, I began to realise some powerful things.

For example: if my thoughts are all negative, I will create more negative experiences. When I was sending out negative radio signals, they attracted negative events and things to me. When I sent out positive radio signals attached to positive feelings and emotions, I started to create positive things in my life.

So, I started to play around with this idea — and it transformed my life.

I played with manifesting car spaces, with romantic relationships, and with creating more and bigger sales at work. It worked. I created one of the biggest sales I've ever had, bringing me a lot of money and prestige within the company. There is a 'but' coming — you have to be careful what you wish for!

It became clear that, if I didn't attach a *feeling* to my thought, I created nothing and it didn't work. Some people have achieved amazing things through their desires and determination. Because they become passionate about it, they have automatically attached their emotions. It consumes them. For most of us in our everyday lives, if we are realistic in what we want we will achieve it — but you must not forget to feel the emotion that is attached to it. Try asking in advance for something special, and don't forget to say 'thank you' when you get it after you've finished laughing because it works!

Once I became aware that we create our own lives by what we think about ... the reality of that was enormous. Everything is energy! As quantum physics now proves, *our physical world is comprised of wavelengths of energy that respond directly to our thoughts.* When you learn to understand this, and direct this energy, there are no limits to what you can create.

When you switch on a radio to listen to the music, you never question how it works. When you do stop to think about it, you know that there are masts up and down the country and all over the world picking up signals. It is the same with electricity, telephones and televisions: they pick up information that is transmitted in one way or another. You never question this yet it all still works — so, once you learn to accept that there is unlimited potential in your thoughts, you can create whatever you want.

We'll explore this further in Chapter Three ('The Power of Your Mind') and you will see more examples throughout this book, as this is such a huge revelation. Some of my thoughts have created wonderful experiences, which I'd like to share with you.

James Arthur Ray, a philosopher, explained this: 'We live in a vibrational universe — everything is vibration from thought to thing. Science and spirituality both agree that what appears to be empty space is actually a field of unlimited consciousness and potential.'

Science and spiritual people agreeing — what an amazing step forward! I could never explain to friends some of the things that have happened to me, because they used to say: 'Prove it,' and I couldn't. However, I would ask them to prove that it *didn't* happen and *they* couldn't!

There is a film called *What the Bleep Do We Know?* where top scientists explain the quantum physics theory. This is worth watching if you want to learn more about the science aspect at a later stage.

Many people are now realising the truth of the concept that you can 'think for' what you want. The film *The Secret* has created tremendous interest. Not everyone has achieved the success they thought it would bring. *The Secret,* through the book, film and DVD, has reached out to many people who would not normally think like this — but the golden nuggets of this film and book seem to be hidden. Some people feel it concentrates more on financial gain than on spiritual freedom. To be rich and powerful would not be possible for the entire world. Many people still don't see how it can work, nor understand how to apply the concepts to themselves; they dismiss it as the latest fad.

There are now quite a few films on this subject, including one called *The Opus* which is a follow-on from *The Secret* and provides the missing link. (Oh yes, there *was* a missing link, which I hope to explain in more detail throughout this book!)

You may also have heard about *cosmic ordering*. Noel Edmonds changed his whole life and career by manifesting what he wanted. In fact, cosmic ordering is an ancient practice. For thousands of years, our ancestors have used abundance creation through ceremony, dance or prayer to create rain, fertile crops, healing and good fortune — so this isn't new. It is just that, over time, enlightened people and new-age thinkers have realised that you can manifest the situations, experiences and materials that you want. There is more about this in Chapter Three.

The philosophy behind both of these ideas is a good way to describe what was happening to me: it is all to do with energy (and more)

… but I do get cross when 'experts' say that we can manifest anything and all the wonderful things we want in just a few days or months! It doesn't work like that.

I was about to find out that there was more to it than simply sending out a request to the Universe, especially where my love life was concerned. It can take weeks, months or even years — but the principles behind these thoughts are correct. They will manifest when the time is right and if the request is right for you. Don't forget also that you can request things which are wrong … your thoughts are far more powerful than you realise.

Of course it is hard to understand how the Universe works, and I am not sure that we ever will understand it fully. However, once you understand the principles the concept makes sense. There is far more to life than merely creating wealth and having brilliant or negative experiences — because there is a reason why you are here. For example, it is unrealistic to think that cosmic ordering alone will make you a millionaire or can find your soul mate. If your life here on Earth is meant to teach you something else, these things will never happen.

My quest for knowledge via networking

Have you noticed that people often come into your life for a reason, just when you need them to help you to grow to the next stage?

I had attended a *Mind Body Soul* exhibition, which I found interesting, and I mentioned this to a friend and colleague Lesley Greenwood. She told me that she knew the owner, Julie, and would introduce me to her. Julie and I gelled instantly; as I was between jobs at the time, she invited me to work with her. Julie and I have since become close friends.

By now I was beginning to have a foot in both worlds. I started to meet other people with whom I could talk about this and who didn't think me odd. On the contrary, I thought some of *them* were a bit odd or weird!

The field of Mind Body Spirit is huge, and attracts people from all walks of life. The people at the events are a diverse mixture of people and therapies. Some have crystal balls, Tarot cards and wear purple, others are what most people would describe as 'normal'. All of them are trying to follow their authentic selves to grow and feel comfortable in their own skins. Each of them is drawn to a particular area which resonates for them, often for their spiritual evolvement.

The perception of *spirituality* has changed over the last few decades, and I think it's because people are now curious to find answers — and organised religion, in its dogmatic way, has pushed people out of the place of worship. I have never believed that I needed to go to a place of worship to embrace spirituality because it has nothing to do with religion.

I realised this when, at the very beginning of my own spiritual awakening, I went to Egypt with a friend Mandy on a luxury cruise down the Nile. Suddenly, in the middle of the night, hundreds of miles from home, I was awakened by a man's voice gently speaking in my ear. I had no idea what he said as I jumped out of bed and said to him: 'How did you know I was here?' Well, of course I can laugh about this now, because where ever we are in the world we are always connected.

Strange as it may seem, at the time I already felt comfortable with the experiences I was having. I wasn't sure why *I* was being privileged to experience these events. It wasn't happening to many of my friends but it was beginning to feel very natural and exciting to me. I was still emotionally screwed up from the death of my parents and my divorce … yet it began to be a huge comfort to know that I was not alone.

We all have different ideas and views on many topics which we find interesting, and I think it is important to talk to people even though we may not always want to follow them. To have a broad picture of what is available in any area of interest, be it Mind Body Spirit, a hobby or a business, helps to broaden your mind. You are never too old to learn and it keeps your mind active and healthy — and helps to keep you young-at-heart and sane.

In my experience, networking is a brilliant way to further yourself and your business. Meeting like-minded people who share a common interest, or people who can help you in some area, is far better than any advertising you can do. It is definitely the way forward in the business world of the twenty-first century.

People are so helpful and give advice away freely. There are many networkers who just want to sell you their product, and most people avoid them, but the vast majority are eager simply to share their knowledge. I have tried various different networking groups, some all women, others are mixed, some in the early hours of the day, some at lunchtime, some in the evening. You'll need to go to as many as you can until you find which you are comfortable with. The best two for me have been The Professional Speakers Association and Ecademy — definitely like-minded people. I have learned an incredible amount from wonderful people there, and I value their friendships.

I also networked at the Mind Body Soul exhibitions — that I was now helping to run – and I made instant friends with some of the people who were running what is known as a *spiritual development circle*. I jumped at the chance to learn more by joining. My growth and knowledge has been amazing, and three of the circle members are now amongst my deepest and closest friends. (In Chapter Eight we'll examine spiritual circles in more detail.)

If you have a hobby or interest it is much nicer when you know like-minded people with whom you can share and bounce around ideas and pass on your knowledge — because when you share with others, you do it with love. Never expect anything in return because what you send out you receive back in abundance in other ways. Often in unexpected ways!

How can you create magical things in your life?

First, I suggest learning to *meditate* as the key to opening up your life. When you have a quiet time to yourself it is beneficial because you are recharging your energy. A deep meditation stimulates the creation of new communication pathways between the logical right brain and the creative left brain. This then balances your brain and gives you a whole-being experience.

So many people think that they haven't got time in their busy lives, that they must do this and that before they could even contemplate spending a bit of quality time on themselves. Taking time out will help you to improve your memory, intuition, creativity and give you much more clarity of thought. It also helps to reduce your stress levels so you come away feeling refreshed, invigorated and more relaxed, allowing you to achieve more. Brilliant ideas will pop into your head, and sometimes the answer to what you have been struggling with or looking for will suddenly come to you.

Meditation doesn't have to last for hours on end — ten to fifteen minutes a day might be all you need. Standing in the shower, sitting in the car when you are early for an appointment, or over a cup of coffee or tea during the day can be just as beneficial. The secret is to let your mind go blank during these times.

There are many different ways to meditate, and various techniques you can learn which are too numerous to mention here — so I will describe a very common and easy to use technique. To learn more about meditation, there are many books and guided meditation CDs available which you could source at your leisure. There is even a light and sound machine called Mindlab™ which may help.

Meditation exercise

The best way to meditate is to concentrate on your breathing. To create the right atmosphere you may wish to light some candles, put on some relaxing music and switch the phone to answering machine. If you have family at home, it might be useful to put a note on your door saying: *DO NOT DISTURB.*

Find a comfortable position, either lying down or sitting upright on the floor or a chair. Some people like to sit in the lotus position, but for beginners that might be uncomfortable — and comfort is the key.

Gently begin to relax your body, from your toes to your shoulders. Take each area of the body separately and be aware of how it feels. Relax your shoulders, then your back — perhaps by sitting further back into your chair. Then notice your stomach, hips, the tops of your legs, your calves, your ankles and then your feet and toes. You may find that your body begins to shift slightly and that you become more stretched than when you started.

Begin to concentrate on your breathing. Take a deep breath in … and then gently breathe out. As you breathe out, send all the negative thoughts out into the Universe at the same time. Keep taking deep breaths for a few minutes, and notice at the same time what your chest is doing. It will be expanding and contracting, which is good. Gradually slow your breathing down to a gentle rhythm, still concentrating on the expansion of your chest. Then play around with your breathing. Make it go faster, then slower, then faster again, and slower again, until you get to a stage when you can hardly feel yourself breathe at all.

What this is doing is taking your mind off the thoughts that will occur to you. When you first start meditating, you may find it impossible to stop things popping into your head; just acknowledge them, and then let them go. You may like to imagine a bubble or balloon wrapped around those thoughts, which you can allow to drift up to the Universe. Perhaps at the very beginning you may like to write your thoughts down, so you stop worrying that you will forget them, and then go straight back to concentrating on your chest and your breathing. By focusing on your breathing, it will help you stop falling asleep — as some people do!

The more you practise this, the easier it will become. The idea is to focus on something other than your thoughts — so, if you find concentrating on your breathing difficult, try focusing on the colour behind your eyelids when they are closed. This may seem odd, because you will be seeing only the colour black; after a time, however, you may find little specks of white popping in, and then gradually little bits of blue or green. Focus on the colours by waiting for the next one to appear, and you may be amazed to find out how long you've been sitting in your chair.

But I would also like to say: *Don't try too hard.* For some people, meditation is difficult and they get cross that they can't do it. When you relax, which is not easy for everyone at first, it will happen much more naturally and you will begin to see the benefits.

As you learn to clear your mind, start talking to yourself in your mind. This is different to the thoughts that will pop in at the start of your meditation. Ask questions in your mind and you may start to have sudden thoughts, hear single words or even see a symbol or vision. Don't worry too much about them, as other words or thoughts may flow in as well. Feel these thoughts, listen to what you feel, sense or even hear in your mind. Your guides and Angels are sending you a message; who knows where this wonderful experience will lead you to?

After you have gently brought yourself back into your space, when your mediation has come to an end, write down everything you felt, what your thoughts were and anything significant that appeared. Keep a diary of your meditations.

You may like to do a meditation where you imagine yourself on a journey walking through some woods or down to the beach. Imagine yourself in a very special place, and then slowly walking along a path; see where it leads you. Let your imagination run away with you and smell the trees and flowers as you walk. Feel the sun on your back. You may even imagine holding a partner's hand while you are doing this. See where it takes you. If you like this idea, there are many guided meditations which may also appeal to you.

Another aspect of meditation occurs when you find yourself having concentrated so hard on something, that the time has just slipped by. Have you ever found yourself lost 'in space' when you are gardening, driving or watching television, when you haven't actually seen anything? This is another form of meditation, as it quietens your mind. It can be beneficial but in a different way.

Some of the symbols you may see can represent interpretations which you may also find come up in dreams. For example, a baby signifies a new beginning; a butterfly or The Statue of Liberty represents freedom; a bird is a messenger; a boat is travel. There are many dream or symbol books where you can look up the meaning to something you have been shown. You will also get to know and have your own interpretations as you develop.

Let's recap...

STEP 1 — Learn to meditate. Find out about synchronicity and read about how your life has opened up to something which is beginning to be amazing. Hopefully you may have begun to realise that there is far more to life than you thought. By embracing some of this information it will lead you to explore more; I hope so, because this can be a wonderful journey.

What are the main things that have made you think? Take some time to consider this: have you experienced any tingling, or started to feel different in some way? Has remembering some of the synchronicity in your life made you realise that perhaps there is more to it? When you start to open your mind you allow some of these experiences into your life: synchronicity may just start to happen more often!

Take some time every day to *stop*. It can be just for a few minutes, if that is all the time you can spare, but use the time to think about how powerful your life is, and could be. You may begin to feel the energy that surrounds you, and to know that you are beautiful as you are right now. Try to meditate for about fifteen minutes a day, and keep a diary.

Wherever you are in life right now, just know that *this is where you are meant to be*. If you believe that you have to change and improve yourself to make yourself successful and happy, don't be surprised to find, as you read on, that this is not so. You already have everything you need inside yourself — it just may need to be unlocked.

The beginning of my awakening

Meditation

Chapter Two

Core Conditioning

People stop and wonder at the height of the mountains,
The depths of the oceans,
And the long course of the rivers
And yet they never stop to wonder about themselves.
— *St Augustine*

To reach where I am today has been a real journey. It has involved soul searching, looking within myself, learning from experiences, gaining more knowledge and generally enjoying the ride.

There have been times when I've been on the top of a mountain, and others when I was at the bottom of the ocean. My emotional merry-go-round has been an eventful ride, something I am sure you can relate to. Along the way I have put up obstacles and knocked down walls, while searching for the meaning to my life. Tears, laughter, fun, joy and love have also played a huge part in this soul searching — and it has been worth every bit of my learning experience. I wouldn't be the person I am today, had I not gone through all these events. My flower has opened and the sweet nectar is now buzzing with bees.

Has *your* flower opened yet? I ask this, because you wouldn't be the person you are today either, if it hadn't been for all the experiences *you* have been through. All of your experiences teach you something different, if you are willing to learn from them. We each have a path to walk — but sometimes it is neither obvious nor easy.

Early on, I began to realise that sometimes you have to go right back to our childhood to see how your life has been and what you have learned. This can give you a real insight into why some things happen in your life. However, it's also important to remember the *good* things you have achieved. Often they get forgotten but they are just as important as the things you regret or feel bad about. (There is more about this in Chapter Four.)

Many people, including myself, find this hard because they can't remember their childhood. Others remember every little detail. In my case, at the age of ten I was in a road accident which fractured my skull — so my memory before then is virtually blank. It is only through chatting to my sisters that I have been able to recall the little details.

The major events which I will mention in a moment *have* stayed with me. Did I block my childhood out because something major happened then? I'm not sure but I don't think so; I have never felt a need to revisit those memories. I just have a feeling of enjoying those times — apart from a few events — and I wonder whether undergoing a hypnotic regression would help me. Who knows? Certainly, for many people, this can be of enormous benefit.

Our childhood influences and memories often play a crucial role in our adult soul-searching. Some people need to let go of the past so that they can live fully in the present. This is not always easy, as I will explain further on, but you may need to *forgive*, *forget* and *move on*. Your hang-ups are like little demons clinging to your mind, and they keep reappearing when you least expect them. However, they can also be your friends because they teach you so much.

When I run workshops I always start with this idea, because our childhood has such a big impact on our lives. Some of the people within a seminar group will have had major trauma in either childhood or later life — but they will have reached a crossroads and are now ready to move on. That's why they are drawn to attend the workshop. During the session, I persuade people to share their successes — but they are not always forthcoming, and sometimes I have to coax it out of them.

As a nation, we have been brought up with the belief that to talk about anything we have achieved is 'boasting'. So, we keep quiet. This is wrong. We should be proud, and learn to walk with pride. We should constantly remind ourselves of our achievements.

In the workshop group, nearly everyone has something to share. Often there are amazing stories to tell. Exclamations such as *How did you do that?* and *Wow that's amazing!* follow these stories, along with cheering and congratulations.

A person who attended one of my workshops, and who has turned her own life around, is my hairdresser, Joe. Over a period I had been coaching and supporting her — but I have known and watched her grow up since she was eleven years old. She had been through a terrible trauma with her daughter, yet now she is inspiring others.

Joe's daughter, at the age of twelve, was groomed and raped by an old man whom she trusted and thought was her friend. Over a series of many months, this man did unmentionable things to her (and to one of her friends) but the child was too frightened to tell anyone. Instead, she started taking hard drugs to blank things out. She broke down after being bullied at school, and at last told her parents — which almost shattered their marriage.

But Joe was her daughter's strength and I am proud of her. She proved to be the backbone of the whole family. The man was eventually sent to jail for a very long time. Joe's daughter's recovery has been a slow painful process but with the help from support agencies she is doing well, even attending college.

At the workshop session, my hairdresser revealed that she was about to embark on a Counselling course so that she can help others who are going through a similar experience. Joe realised that she had grown into a woman whom she never thought she would be. The childhood experiences will stay with her daughter forever but she is growing into a beautiful young lady with an inner strength *she* never realised she had.

As a mentor for the Prince's Trust, I am working with a young girl, whom I will call Mary, who has just come out of local authority care. She is having to fend for herself in what seems to her a big scary world, and her past traumas will go with her into the next stage of her life. Working to overcome what Mary calls her *angers against life* is hard for her, and recently she has started self-harming for the first time. Gradually she is learning to deal with things but she was very reluctant at first. She couldn't understand why I or anyone else cared what happened to her.

Mary's is a terribly sad story. So many dysfunctional people in her life had turned their own problems into hers. She felt an enormous burden, having to watch her family drink themselves into oblivion; they couldn't be bothered to work and had no purpose other than self pity. Mary's family were a fine example of how *not* to be a role model. Of course, they couldn't help it; that was the only means they had to cope with their sad lives.

We all affect each other with our actions, role modelling and the standards by which we live.

Everyone has a past. It can take years to overcome some of the events that have happened — but it *can* be the most empowering thing you'll ever do. You can overcome anything and move your own mountain if the desire is strong enough. But only you can make it happen.

Sometimes it demands ruthless honesty and the willingness to face your inner demons. Equally, it is about valuing every part of yourself, as the beautiful person you were when you were born.

Peeling the onion

Before you start to look at your childhood, I want you to remember something as you read ahead:

Only *you* know what your experiences have been like. Only *you* felt the emotions of all that has happened to you, good and bad, throughout your life. You may have shared and talked about certain things, you may have thought back before now to certain events, but only *you* truly know how they have affected you, deep within your core being — your true self. No-one else has experienced your life, and other people can only know the snippets of information that you have given them.

Everyone's life is so different because we each come here for different reasons, to learn different lessons. That is why you are unique. That is also why you should never judge others. We each come into this world on our own, as an individual soul, and we leave this world on our own. Along the way you will meet people who can keep you company and teach you things so that you can grow. But what you do with your life is up to you — that is why you have free will.

Please also know that there is not another copy of you anywhere else in the world. How amazing is that!

My own grounding

My parents supported me and my three sisters as we were growing up, in a way that I am deeply grateful for. I was the black sheep of the family, always getting into mischief. To me, school was more about socialising and playing sports than learning — and I was expelled from two schools and one college. Although I loved sport and was very good at lacrosse and hockey, I could not see the point of algebra and some other subjects. It is not something I'm proud of but it is not something which I have ever put on my CV either!

They must have despaired but my parents never let me see it. Instead, they always helped me move on to the next opportunity which opened up elsewhere. I am grateful for that now — but at the time I thought that was how everyone was raised. My parents always said that if we were not top of the class, then as long as we did our best, and were polite and respectful, then that was more important. They used to say sometimes that they were disappointed in us, which was far more powerful than any punishment they could have given us.

But my senior schooling did have a big impact on me and affected me for many years. My parents were keen for us to go to boarding school as they felt we would get a better education — but I had other ideas. Perhaps if I'd known, at age eleven, where they were sending me it might have helped me adjust. Had I been an avid reader of the books by Enid Blyton or the stories about St Trinians, I might have thought that this experience was going to be fun, and gone willingly.

My Mum took me up to London to buy a school uniform which consisted of some very odd clothing! We had to wear a cloak and a straw boater hat, which made me wonder what this new place was going to be like. We also had to buy a trunk to fit this all in. The trunk was sent on ahead of me, and my Mum then took me up to one of the big London railways stations where she introduced me to a lady who she said would take care of me. She then casually said: 'Goodbye dear, see you soon,' and walked away.

I had no idea where I was going or what to expect from all these strangers — kids and adults — waving frantically, some crying, some laughing and all shouting and wearing this very odd uniform. I can now relate to the young Harry Potter, as my own dungeon was about to be revealed.

The school had strange dormitories. I shared mine with thirty other girls, with no privacy other than a curtain. There was bullying; I remember at one early stage having my head flushed in a toilet! The reason for this treatment eludes me now but was very traumatic at the time. I got the slipper whacked across my bum in the headmistress's office on many occasions. If my misdemeanour wasn't too serious, a wooden blackboard duster was tapped across my knuckles.

My trouble was that I talked too much, both in and out of class. I am also the sort of person who will do anything for anyone if you *ask* me — but if you *tell* me to do it, a chill runs up my spine and I rebel. I think this is where I learned to be an individual, strong person; otherwise I would have floundered.

Did my Mum shed tears as she walked away? I have never known. She was brought up to keep a stiff upper lip, in a well-to-do family who found it hard to show emotion. I do know that *I* felt unwanted; all I wanted was to be at home with my friends, playing in the street and going to the local school together on the bus.

By the age of eighteen I wanted to spread my wings and have some fun, so I travelled and thumbed my way around Europe for three years with a group of five other girls. That taught me a lot about life. It was a wonderful experience, something unusual for people to do in the late 1960s and early 70s. We had a ball!

We experimented with all aspects of life — boys, light drugs, booze and the high life — but we never had any real money. Although we worked, we also starved to keep thin. We were all very sensible and returned to real life as much wiser girls; we're still close friends today, over forty years later. Nowadays it is common for students to take a gap year; I think that's brilliant but it is not for everyone.

Having been expelled, I never took an exam or passed any GCSEs (as they were known in those days). This has never stopped me landing any job that I have wanted throughout my entire working career. But it did come back to haunt me, and was one of my biggest fears when my whole life changed four years ago.

I thought about applying to the College of Psychic Studies in London, to give some talks and run some workshops. I looked them up on the Internet, only to discover the most terrifying application form I had ever seen. I had to list all my qualifications, exams results, diplomas, experience and a whole lot more!

This was a huge stumbling block; surely I wasn't qualified to teach others if I didn't have that 'piece of paper' which so many people now expect of us. Years ago, you could walk in and out of jobs like hopping on a bus.

But synchronicity was to play a role again a year later when I attended a workshop run by a friend, Mindy Gibbins-Klein, the book midwife. Guess who I was partnered up with? Max Eames, President of the College of Psychic Studies. We hit it off straight away, and had a laugh about his dreaded application form. Of course I don't need to fill it in now ... I know the boss!

In fact, Max and I are now working together on a number of projects. We both realised that our meeting was going to prove far more beneficial to us both than we initially thought. I had managed to forget about the application form, by releasing the idea to the Universe, so when we met it was very unexpected. I realised then that sometimes the Universe brings far better results than we can imagine.

What I had mentally done was let go of my resistance to give *spiritual* talks, rather than just personal development seminars. This is called 'detaching' from the end result. Once I decided that this would be my way forward, 'they' opened doors way beyond my expectations. Synchronicity plays a huge part in our lives if you allow it and notice it. Many more doors opened too, which I will tell you about later.

This fear of mine set me back for over a year. I earned no money because of it. Friends and colleagues were surprised at me, and told me how silly I was being. However it was a friend, Nick Williams, who has written many books on this subject, who coached me back to having the confidence I'd had as a teenager. I could relate to Nick because he had been there himself and overcome his own fear and gradually liberated himself from many of the limiting beliefs and attitudes he had grown up with. He now has a fabulous career travelling all over the world helping others learn to do the job that is their life's calling.

As he said: 'Sheila, your experiences in life have taught you so much and are far more powerful than any qualification on a piece of paper. You speak and teach from your heart and with such passion. Some people who have studied for years have no depth to their soul like you.' I can now say *Thank you Nick*, as I shall be eternally grateful to him.

I have to say that I could see all this in others but not in myself. Many of the wonderful people I have met who have brilliant careers now have been self-made, former drop-outs with not a qualification to their name. What they all possess, which I have too, are confidence and determination.

Did you know that Winston Churchill failed the qualifying exams for three years running when trying to enter Sandhurst? Or that Thomas Edison was once at the bottom of his class? Albert Einstein flunked Maths and was called 'mentally slow', and Henry Ford was written off by one teacher as 'a student who shows no promise' — so there's hope for us all!

Point To Ponder

- Do you know anybody who fits the bill as an Entrepreneur, who is self-made? Richard Branson comes to mind as an example.
- What are the qualities you admire in such people? How could you grow if you learned some of their strategies?
- If, like me, you have never passed any exams, how could you overcome the stigma you feel?
- I realised some time ago that everyone starts their life journey from the bottom of the mountain. No-one starts at the top! (Or if they do, often they fall hard.)
- How can you not feel worthy within yourself? You were created as a perfect human specimen — so what can have gone wrong? Did outside influences tell you something different about yourself?
- Could something inside you… something alive and powerful… be blocking your path? Is your own core conditioning setting you up to resist personal growth?

Conditioning

There are several types of conditioning, any or all of which may affect us in life.

- Childhood and parental modelling
- Educational imprinting
- Media and films — outside influences

- Organised religion
- Our own (and our significant others') doubts/fears/guilt

Let's take a stroll down Memory Lane. You, as a little bundle of joy, came into the world full of innocence, hopes and dreams. All you needed was to be loved, fed, cuddled and to be kept warm and safe.

We have no idea what our lives in the future are going to be like — but we all come here for a reason, and we are all powerful beautiful human beings. Some say that we choose our parents because of the lessons they can teach us, and that we pre-plan our life before we are even born but as we develop we forget. Sometimes I think this can be a good thing, because we might want to go back to where we came from if we knew what lay ahead!

Did you know that your parents hadn't gone to a school to learn how to bring you up? I am sure most parents always do what they think best and often simply replicate how they were brought up themselves. That is usually all they know.

The world is becoming a multi-cultural society and of course we all have our morals and disciplines which we inherit from our own parents and cultures. However, sometimes the little things in your childhood, or even the bigger experiences, can have a profound effect upon you.

You have no idea at the time how you are being affected. Everyone thinks their own upbringing is normal and assumes that everyone else is going through the same things. How wrong that is.

As a baby, you gradually grew and learned new skills at each stage of your development. When you learned to crawl and then walk, your parents or carers were probably delighted and said how clever you were. Their happiness and love sounded in their voices, so you were delighted too. Falling over was something natural, and they ran to pick you up and give you a cuddle to brush away your tears. Or perhaps you were told that you were a 'baby' if you cried so you had to keep that quivering lip still.

Then you became more interested in the world around you and wanted to explore. You were also learning to talk. The word *no* seemed very interesting to you, as it always brought a reaction! But you were also learning that you can't do things. *'No, don't do that', 'Oh for heaven's sake stop it', 'Leave me alone as I'm busy, go away', 'You're stupid, why on earth did you do that?'* Sometimes these words would be screamed at you when your parents were stressed. They are often not meant to hurt. But when they are said over and over again, they stick. In time they become believable, and then believed. They become ingrained in your subconscious mind.

Then you go to school — not always a pleasant experience. You are not top of the class so you must be stupid. Why aren't you doing better? You're trying your hardest but your siblings may have excelled but you haven't. You hate sports and dread getting changed in the changing rooms, let alone run around a pitch. But your friends like it so what is wrong with you?

You're being *compared*. Can you relate to this and see what is beginning to happen?

Then the excitement of Father Christmas turns into reality, and you realise that perhaps your parents had lied to you or that something wonderful is only make-believe. Think back and remember how you felt at the time of finding that this wonderful experience was not real. You may have lain awake the following Christmas Eve, waiting to see what happened, trying to catch out your parents — which was fun. The world was becoming a confusing place!

It may not have affected you at all because you half-knew already. However, the point I am making is that your childhood holds many wonderful memories but also some damaging ones.

Our childhood is the beginning of our conditioning.

When you were young, you had hopes and dreams about what you wanted to do when you grew up. I wanted to be a nurse and be like Mother Theresa … or an archaeologist! How many of you wanted to be a doctor, airline pilot or air hostess or fly to the moon in a space shuttle? I bet not many will have dreamed of being a drain cleaner unless their father did something like that. (Sorry, to any cleaners reading this, it's just meant as an example.)

You might also have believed in fairies living at the bottom of your garden. Or if you were naughty the demons would come and get you.

Praise, on the other hand, is a wonderful experience and encouragement. Praise should be at the top of everyone's list of things to do. To be praised helps you tackle the daunting things you are going to encounter later on in life. Praise gives you a belief in yourself which can last a lifetime. Children who are praised often will go much further in their careers and personal lives, armed with confidence and a lack of fear.

Point To Ponder

- Can you relate to any of the above? Which experiences had the most dramatic impact on you?

- Does this conditioning still resonate with you or have you let it go?

Parental modelling

How many of us in childhood heard the words: *Money is the root of all evil. Only the rich get the luxuries in life. You don't deserve that. It's all right for some. To do good works you must go without.* But the really interesting one is: *Money doesn't grow on trees.* There's an argument for saying it *does* because paper is made from trees!

There are many sayings which lead some of us to believe that to earn or have a lot of money is wrong. In my opinion the most damaging one is: 'You don't deserve…' One of my most profound moments occurred when the reality behind those statements hit home.

The Yes Group runs inspired personal development evenings once a month in the UK and Internationally, featuring dynamic speakers from around the world. I went to one of their meetings one evening, and heard a fabulous speaker called Randy Gage explain about his life. His humour and the examples he gave made everyone laugh … more importantly, he made us *think*.

Randy had been brought up in America. He lived in a rough neighbourhood which was violent and very poor. Everyone around him had a negative attitude to life. When he was a teenager he was in jail — but then he decided he didn't want to live like that any more.

So, he took drastic action and moved thousands of miles away to start a new life. Not everyone would want to do that, not everyone would be able to, and it was a fundamental turning point in his life. Randy consciously wanted to change, knowing that if he didn't he would end up back in jail. He wanted to enjoy his life instead, and earn lots of money like the people he only heard about and saw on television. No-one he knew had done anything like this but he believed in himself and his *want* far outweighed the *how*.

Randy surrounded himself with like-minded people and made new friends. He rose from working in many dead-end jobs to become a multi-millionaire — but his first company collapsed and he lost it all. So, he picked himself up and over a period of time founded another company which became worth millions. To cut his story short, he then sold the company which had made him rich.

After that, he then took a different angle to life and started sharing with others his philosophy on life. Randy is now a very well respected speaker and motivator, known as *The Millionaire Messiah*. His message is that, not only are you meant to be rich, but that it is a sin to be poor! He travels the world teaching that health, happiness, and wealth are possible for anyone who desires them.

One of the most profound things he said is: 'If I didn't have all this money, I could not travel and share with millions of people around the world that they could do this too. If I had stayed poor, I would have only been able to share my success and strategies with a handful of people.' How very true.

He went on to say that he can only go back for one night at a time, to visit his old friends and family — because they still have a negative attitude and he doesn't want to be drawn back into that energy. Randy Gage is just one of the many people who are living proof that you can change your life if you have the determination, mind set and willingness to overcome whatever obstacles are put in front of you.

His lesson to us at the talk was that we each have a choice. You choose which one you would rather be:

V versus V versus V   =   Victim or Victor is your Vision

We all deserve to earn money — but don't keep it all for yourself. The Universe will provide you with everything you need if you are not greedy, work hard and share with others. Teaching is a wonderful experience. Charity work, sharing your knowledge, or even just supporting a friend in need with your time is all part of sharing your wealth.

Wealth is not just *money*. To have personal wealth is precious beyond measure.

How can you overcome negative thoughts and words?

Negative thoughts and words are like a virus in the brain. They need to be cleared by changing your core conditioning and beliefs.

Let's begin with words and actions:

The word *can't* does not appear in the English dictionary! So, why do we say it to ourselves so often? The little bit at the end of a lot of words (n't) changes the whole meaning.

Should (n't)   Could (n't)   Can (n't)   Do (n't)   Have (n't)

Then there are the phrases:

If only. Because of. I never. I have to. And that lovely word — *But…*

Take those words out of your mindset and you change your thought patterns and visions. Learn these few words instead: ***I can….. as nothing is impossible!***

Let's turn some of those negative words around:

- I *can't* do that…   What I *can* do is…
- That's a good idea *but*…   That's a good idea *and if I*…
- *If* I achieve…   *When* I achieve…
- I *should* do…   I *could* do…

A similar magic can transform negative phrases:

- There's nothing I can do   Let's consider the options
- If only…   I want to…
- I have to…   I choose to

- I can't motivate my…   I haven't found a way yet but I will
- It's difficult to…   It's not so easy...
- That's impossible   There is always a way
- I don't want to…   Maybe I could ….
- I don't like…   I may dislike but…
- I'm not that type of person   I choose what I do in my life
- Why has this happened to me? What can I learn from this?
- I never…   I haven't yet…..
- I'm no good at…   If I want to get better at…, I can learn how

Of course, it would be wrong to say that, merely by thinking positively, you can suddenly climb Mount Everest or fly a plane. However, if you have the ability and are prepared to work at it, the possibility is there! There's an awesome thought to dwell on.

Tip

- It's interesting just to listen to yourself when you speak, while you're going about your normal day. You may be surprised how many times in a day you say negative words to yourself and other people. Once you become conscious of your self talk, your whole world can change.

Outside conditioning

Media and films, education and religion are outside influences that can affect us deeply.

Love is the most powerful creation on Earth. I find it hard to embrace the idea that poverty, war and all the destruction that is going on around us is not Man-made. Most wars are created by the power of Man. Often war is about whose religion is right, and so often it seems that hardship is acceptable for others. I touch on this subject now, only because I get so cross when people claim that outside influences don't affect people.

Thinking about this realistically — watching horror or violent movies, seeing people shooting each other, being brought up in a faith which teaches that punishment for ourselves and others is necessary — how can all this be done in the name of love and good for us all?

The media also tell us that you have to be thin to be acceptable, and that you mustn't let yourself get old. No-one seems to mention that inside yourself, the person you are, is where to find the beauty that we are all searching for. It doesn't matter that you may not conform to what others say you should be like — that is what makes each of us unique — but we are all far too worried about what others think.

Why do some people love to have power over others? Is it about fear or control? You also see such violence everywhere, on television, in the cinemas, in comics and newspapers; to our children this is becoming a normal way of life! Then they re-enact and play on their computers and Playstations, and they become those people. Children are often bullied because of perceived differences from their peers. Bullying has always been a big part of many children's (and adults') lives, where power over others again comes into play — but as a society is this what we really want? Thankfully, many people are now standing up and saying that this has got to stop.

Too many children around the world are orphans and suffer from poverty, starvation, AIDS, governmental greed and natural disasters. They have seen horrors beyond description and live hard and brutal lives. Their parents suffer too. Global warming is not the only destruction causing some of this.

What we do in the West affects people on the other side of the world. What you do affects others around you too, but often you don't realise it. If you can learn not to be so selfish, you can help others who have lives less fortunate than your own.

There is good and bad in every society. There always has been and there always will be, until the day comes when we all learn to love each other. On that day, I trust, when greed and power subside and people become more spiritually aware of what astrologers call *The Age of Aquarius* which emphasises on humanity, kindness, truth, spirituality and enlightenment — all things you can find within yourself — this will all dovetail beautifully into a single global vision of peace and hope.

Perhaps you need to ask yourself: what about all the children who do lovely things but *don't* get special television programmes made about them? There are children all over the world who don't fight and are not in gangs. They don't vandalise their housing estates, and they do respect their elders. Why aren't we shouting about *them* and telling *their* stories?

Many adults, and not just the famous, are standing up and speaking out about changing this world and highlighting the destruction we are wreaking upon the planet every day. There are many people working behind the scenes to create a world full of love and where we all become equal. There are now a few films highlighting this, one of the most powerful ones I have seen being *The Shift*. For those who wish to take the ideas in the film further, there is a movement attached to it.

Television and our newspapers are full of negative news, and we only occasionally promote the wonderful people in our society. Occasionally a TV station, local or national newspaper praises a heroic person or event — and then you turn the page and read that someone has been killed. Where is the sense in all this? Stop reading a newspaper or watching the news for a month and you will be amazed how uplifted you begin to feel.

Love, kindness and basic human rights are too often forgotten. Does it really matter whose Universal Source you believe in or which faith you follow? Assuming there is a God, Buddha, Allah or whatever other entity you believe created this world, do you think they would want bloodshed, poverty and hardship to be what this world is all about? I don't think so.

Yet, that is exactly how so many people are living their lives. We often wonder what difference it would make if we were to change something in our own lives, because in the bigger picture our own small action would not change anything. Of course, if everyone felt like that, then nothing would ever change. But each person's thoughts and actions *can* affect the world.

By spreading peace, love and humanity you can begin to change things. Every thought you have reflects somewhere else in the world (In Chapter Three there is more about this) because we are all connected. If you spread love to those closest to you, you begin to spread it across the globe because they will then share their love with others around them. If you can radiate love to everyone you know, family, friends and work colleagues — even strangers in the street can be given a smile — this will then spread around the world as each one passes it on.

Greed and envy are destructive. So many people feel that they need to have everything: a bigger house, more money ... but money can *not* buy happiness. What these people are doing is looking to the outside world to give them happiness — and it can only be found deep within yourself, in your core being.

Have you ever dreamed of buying something, gone and bought it, and then suddenly you wanted even more because it hadn't given you what you thought it would?

Money

It can buy you a house — but never a home
It can buy you a clock — but not time
It can buy you a position — but not respect
It can buy you a bed — but not sleep
It can buy you a book — but not knowledge
It can buy you medicines — but not health
It can buy you acquaintances — but never friends
It can buy you blood — but not life
It can buy you sex — but not love
— Chinese Proverb

Some cultures seem to have more peace, love and soul in their tribes and religious faiths than we in the West will ever have. Greed and material possessions seem to have taken over — and yet we try to cultivate those cultures to suit our ways. Why should we assume our way to be the better one? Perhaps we should learn lessons from those cultures; their people may suffer from hunger in their bodies but we here in the West seem to be suffering from hunger in our souls.

They can teach us so much about love, family unions and supporting each other. Some tribes do have some traditions and customs which we find horrific and which we will never understand. They may be starved of material possessions and medicines. Their sanitary conditions may be appalling. Yet, deep inside, they have a faith which is not parallel with our own.

Yes, I too believe — as I'm sure most of the western world believes — that we can and should help those peoples with our technology, knowledge and skills. But they too can help *us*.

The spirit of our souls seems to be dying inside us. We don't challenge ourselves any more because the greed and selfishness overrides that peaceful feeling towards which we all strive. Why is *power* so powerful? Power can be such a destructive thing ... and why should we not all be equal? Men and women should be equal — and if we go far enough back in history, they were. But then Man and Religion decided *they* wanted to control the world.

We each have different roles to play in life but we are all still equal.

Something To Think About

- The films that you watch — are they all violent? How would you feel about watching something funny or educational instead?

- Your education — if you were not top of the class did it really matter? Think of your other qualities. We all have so much more potential than we are led to believe.

- Your religion — shouldn't it be about sharing the love you have, for yourself and others? Many religions are. But some can be cruel, with punishments and rules which must be abided by or else. Religion can be an open or a closed door into spirituality — and spirituality goes far beyond religion.

- The magazines you read — do remember that all models are airbrushed and in real life may not be as wonderful as you think. Is the gossip in magazines really necessary? Do you really want to know what everyone else is doing, so you can compare yourself and feel miserable that you haven't got what they have?

Go back to your childhood, when you were running barefoot in the sand, laughing and giggling, running in and out of the sea, building sand castles or playing games on the beach or by a river:

- Did your parents or carers help, or did they just sit back and watch you?
- Did you like danger and dirt, dressing up, or painting and drawing? Use your imagination and long term memory to recall those days.
- Was there a teacher who had a great influence in your life? Have you ever traced him or her to say thank you and tell them what you have achieved?

Then go back to your teenage years:

- Remember all the brilliant things you did.
- Who were the people in your life then, and how did they influence you?
- Go back to remembering Brownies or Cubs, dance or drama lessons. Were you taught a musical instrument? Did you go to church, play out on the street with all your friends? Remember all the wonderful things that you achieved. Did you pass your driving test first time? Think about your first job, your first boyfriend/girlfriend. When you get a moment, dig out your old photos and look at the faces of the people who mean most to you. You may even like to re-read your old love letters and Valentine cards if you still have them.

There is something I have done, which many people who visit my house spend ages admiring. It's a collage of all my old photographs. Rather than keeping them shut away in a drawer or a box, I cut them out and pieced them together, overlapping the pictures. It makes a sensational talking point. I have made one collage for my family and childhood, and the other is for friends and my life now.

Perhaps this is something you would like to do. Old photographs can be a brilliant reminder of the good things and people in our lives.

Your conditioning

Do you have any *core conditioning* that may be blocking you? Take your time to think deeply about this; you may need to go back to your early childhood or teenage years. You may also like to look more deeply at your religious beliefs (if you have them) because they may not be aligned with your views in this present day. Also, think about how you can change your mind set by releasing and letting go of your old thought patterns and memories without doubt or fear or guilt.

Whatever it is, or whoever it may be, let it or them go. They're in the past and they're holding you back. *There is nothing you can do to change them* and it may be something which you are repeating now, to yourself or perhaps to your family. This sort of thing can eat away at you and even make you ill. You are only destroying and hurting yourself.

It is true that words, actions or beliefs can hurt; sometimes words said to you can be very cruel. But often, words come out of a person's mouth before they think! If at the time you were only a child, maybe that person was wrong; they should have been more understanding to *you* — not the other way around. It is important to think about the perception of how that person (or the experience) made you feel.

Sometimes Inner Child Therapy work can be helpful. Childhood traumas are often ignored, or swept under the carpet, by adults. Family bereavements were seldom explained to children as recently as a few years ago; therefore the child's feelings were never validated or dealt with at the time. This can be crippling and the confusion may carry through to adulthood — which is why it should be addressed. Talking to a therapist can lift the sadness which may have stayed with you all this time, and may set you free from your hidden agenda.

If it is more serious, such as abuse or bullying, then forgive that person because they probably knew no better. They might well have been abused or bullied themselves; you often find that someone who bullies has a very unhappy home life themselves. They are not in control of their own situation, so they want to control *you*.

I learned this when my daughter was bullied at school. Many years later, when her attacker was in her mid-twenties, she confessed that her father had been sexually abusing her at the time, and she was threatened not to tell anyone. For years she lived on three biscuits a day. We'd had no idea. Her anorexia prevented her from having her own children, and she was then jealous of my daughter when her baby was born.

Sometimes a difficult childhood can help build a strong character within you, as you don't need others' approval. It can help you become more self-sufficient and independent, allowing you to find your own direction without relying on other people. It makes you aware of what others are experiencing and develops your compassion — but it can also be a lonely place.

So, is your circle of conditioning still going around? The beautiful thing about *letting go* is that it creates the space for magical new things to flow into your life that are more fully aligned with the person that you are now, are becoming, or wish to become. Say goodbye to it by acknowledging it and learning from it — but it's time to move on.

Tip

A good way to do this is write it *all* down on a piece of paper. You can do this in a number of ways. Either write a letter to yourself or to a particular person, and open your heart. Or list everything, and then either fold it and put it somewhere safe or burn it. By burning it you are releasing it to the Universe and saying, *I don't need this anymore, so please take the weight off my shoulders.* Watch those little pieces blow in the wind.

I do this at the end of October, at a time called Samhain (pronounced *Shaveen*). I burn all the things I want to disappear, that I may be holding on to and want to let go. Six months later in May, at a time called Bealtaine (pronounced *Beltaine*), I write down all the nice things I want to bring into my life.

You could do this at any time you like — but it can be more powerful on these spiritual occasions.

Fear of failure and fear of success

A fear of failure is a recognised condition that we fully accept may happen to us when we want to try something new. Sometimes you may feel a failure. But there is also an often unrecognised concept of *fear of success*.

You may never have realised that fear of success is happening to you. Perhaps self-doubt and prostination have set in and you are not sure why. I will cover this more in Chapter Seven — but I am mentioning it here because it is something that also resonates with your core conditioning.

In your subconscious or conscious mind, something may be causing doubt in connection with your sense of self-worth. Do you deserve success? Will your friends be jealous? Will they still talk to you? How will you deal with all the success that your new venture will bring you? Should you take a chance and follow your dream?

Sometimes when you want to do something different, which may not be aligned to what your friends or family are doing, you stop yourself out of fear of what others will think. But we are each on a different journey, each with different wants and ideas. Outside influences *can* have a huge impact on you — but *you* might be ready to move on while they are not, so you should resist those outside influences. Each of us goes through different stages at different times, and to hold back on your own success will just frustrate you. If they are true friends they will be supportive.

This can be hard to deal with. Your core resistance sets in, creating yet another barrier to cross.

Nick Williams, in his book *The Work We Were Born To Do*, explains this very well. He says: 'All of us have been born with unique gifts and talents, but most of us have not been taught or encouraged to find, develop or express those qualities; we may even have been rewarded for hiding or denying them.'

Fear of success can be just as frightening and real as any other limiting condition.

I can relate to fear of success myself because of my self-doubt over those paper qualifications that I didn't have. I kept asking myself, *Do I deserve success? Am I worthy? Am I deluding myself that I could make a difference?* Fear and power may be two completely different aspects of life — but each in its own way can take hold of you.

Point To Ponder

- Can you remember a time when you were frightened of succeeding?
- How did you overcome the invisible parrot that sat on your shoulder, telling you that you were foolish to try? Is it still there?
- Do you wake up in the night with cold sweats?
- Thinking about your fear makes it worse. Instead, concentrate on the end result that you desire, and the fear will slip away — over time.
- Your reality is how you react to the situations around you.

You fear change because it is easier to stay in your comfort zone, than to change something and risk that it doesn't work or that you might fail. Sometimes you give up too soon, because of setbacks — but even setbacks bring the useful lesson of how not to do something. Setbacks do *not* mean you should give up. You often let change go because something doesn't happen instantly, the way the media tells us all to expect.

Your comfort zone has been with you since childhood — but if you want to succeed you may have to step outside that comfort zone and face your fears. Fear and resistance are major obstacles, and it is frightening to overcome them. Once you recognise that they are holding you back, you are halfway there.

It's important also to change your *perception* of your fears and problems because they limit your beliefs and hold you back.

Asking for help is something with which many people struggle — myself included! I find this difficult for two reasons. Firstly, I am a bit too independent and believe I can do everything myself. Secondly, I don't like to bother someone else or take up their time.

But I have learned that people are generally willing to share their knowledge and help when they can. I am always willing to do it for others, so why wouldn't they for me? Rather than struggle over something, which can take me hours, days or even weeks, I've learned that a colleague or friend has the skill to do that particular thing in hours or just a few minutes. That is their expertise.

If I can help anyone I always do. Because of my marketing success, I am always willing to sit down with someone for an hour or so to give them tips and ideas. I get a buzz from it, while they are scribbling their notes. They often have no idea how to market a product or even themselves, and are incredibly grateful to me because I've saved them hours of painful grappling — and because I have helped them to conquer their fears. To me, the time spent is nothing; I enjoy it. Others will enjoy helping you — but you do have to ask. It can be a two-way arrangement, if you can help them at some other time with *your* expertise.

Your body armour is your shell

On a personal level, your protective shell needs to come down occasionally to allow people to help you, or even perhaps just to get to know you. Being more open allows your emotions, feelings and true inner being to come out. Often, people fear how they will be perceived or don't want to worry others if they have problems, so they keep these feelings and thoughts trapped inside.

Keeping up your shell means you are putting up enormous barriers and are not being honest with yourself or others. It can be a lifelong habit, when people are afraid to let down their guard. You may have good reasons for this — but it can be good to let other people help. A good example of this is when someone is ill; friends, neighbours or even family members offer help because they care.

When you see some of the elderly people on television who are living in squalor because they refuse help, it makes you wonder how they've got into such a state. Perhaps it's because they are innately stubborn and independent — but often other people have offered to help and been turned away. The situation gets out of control and then of course the person in need of the help is completely unable to do anything because of the enormity of it. This is another self-protection mode. People genuinely care about each other and give their time freely to help others — but when you need their assistance, it is up to you to let your guard down first and open up.

People put barriers around themselves for many reasons. Sometimes it's because they have been brought up to keep a stiff upper lip. Or there may be sound reasons because something horrible has happened and they have been deeply hurt or frightened, or the culture of their job dictates that it is considered a sign of weakness to talk about feelings. Whatever the reason, it can be a rich and rewarding experience when you do open up and begin to let your guard down.

This recently happened to a friend, Mark. He had suffered a heart attack but kept his feelings about it inside, so as not to scare his family. During the heart attack his spiritual door was opened. He experienced a beautiful sense of peace — but he kept this from everyone he knew because he couldn't comprehend such a 'weird' feeling.

But Mark wanted to learn more. He read every spiritual book he could find. And yet nothing more happened for several years.

Our paths crossed through a business network. On that first occasion I told him only a tiny bit about my spiritual side — but I had no idea of his experience because he said nothing. The day before our second meeting, he unexpectedly had a spiritual experience while he was doing a meditation; he suddenly felt as if someone was pouring love and joy into him, and he was overflowing as this lasted for about an hour. Of course I could help him to understand this. We chatted for hours and I encouraged him to join a spiritual circle to learn more.

Mark chose to attend these twice-monthly gatherings in secret. He wouldn't tell his family, saying they would not understand. However, he continued reading spiritual books so his family must have realised something was going on.

After a while the situation was becoming awkward, as his life was changing in ways he did not understand and therefore could not explain. He had always been an agnostic and cynic, yet here he was sitting in a spiritual circle. But how was he to tell his family? I suggested he write them a letter, since he didn't feel able to tell them face-to-face. Mark liked this idea and he wrote a long letter. He left the letter lying around for his wife and daughter to read while he took the dog for a walk.

When his family read the letter they felt relieved. They'd known *something* was going on, and now that the letter had opened the door they were able to discuss it openly. Mark's wife gave him her blessing.

That letter went on to open even more doors. Mark's Dad was ill, so he shared his secret with his parents. Reading the letter helped his Dad soon afterwards when his time of passing came. It also helped his mother to deal with her own grief and she tells everyone about it.

This man, who had been brought up never to show or talk about his feelings, and who had a career that also required keeping feelings hidden, found that opening up in this way would help him in ways he had never imagined. It helped people around him too. Mark's spiritual journey has also opened up into something amazing as he now has a purpose and inner contentment.

Let's recap…

STEP 1 — Meditate every day.

STEP 2 — Let go of fears, core conditioning and resistance.

One of the most powerful lessons you can learn is that reality is the result of your vision. Your vision is the result of your core fundamental beliefs. And your core fundamental beliefs are what you have programmed into your subconscious mind.

When you change your programming, you also change your core beliefs and vision. It is entirely possible to take down the obstacles you have put up in the past, because life here on Earth isn't meant to be a struggle.

Why do you concentrate so much on negative things, when you could achieve far more and instead bring joy into your life and this world? We all achieve more than we realise — and often it is the poorest people in the world who are the most contented.

Why do you listen to what others say we should be doing, whether in our childhood or as you grow older and outside influences become more apparent? Perhaps it is because you are human beings! None of us should feel guilty about not being perfect; our fears may have created what I call stumbling blocks, but you can have such joy when you begin to awaken to who you really are. You can then approach your full potential and achieve what you were meant to when you first came into this world.

Your past has taught you many things. Now let's move on to your future.

Releasing Core Conditions

Chapter Three

The Power Of Your Mind

What ever the mind can conceive and believe, it can achieve.
— Napoleon Hill, author of Think and Grow Rich

The power within your mind is one of the most amazing things you can use to your advantage because it is connected to your Higher Self. However, it is also connected to the ego — which can be one of the most restricting things. Somewhere, you have to find a balance.

Taking the ego out of the equation can be difficult, as it tends to concentrate on the past and is not interested in the future. One of the big lessons is to learn to 'live in the now' rather than worry about the future.

When you learn to go with your flow, often that is when life opens up so that you no longer need to worry about where life is going. You become more content, and things magically come to you. You become a magnet to all the positive things you think about. And your attitude plays a big role.

I have always believed in positive thinking, plus the right attitude, and in following my intuition. However, it was only when I decided to turn a letter I'd written to my children into a book that the power behind those easy-to-say words turned into magical reality in my life.

After my parents died, I suddenly realised that I had never truly known them. I decided that one day I would write to my own children, so that at least *they* would know and understand who *I* am as a person. I had done a lot with my life of which they knew so little … but the time never seemed quite right to talk about it.

A few years later, I was experiencing difficulties at home with my daughter and a separation from my granddaughter. I handed in my notice at work as I was not performing as well as I should. I couldn't concentrate and spent most of my time in floods of tears. That was a dreadful time for me, my heart truly broken.

I had no other job to go to and at the time I didn't care. Something inside was telling me it was the right thing to do. I can remember driving into work one Monday morning, and it was as if someone was inside the car with me, pushing me forward to hand in my notice. I just followed my gut instinct, without worrying about the future. This is a very scary thing to do but my senses and faith were very powerful, deep within my core being. I had no idea then how powerful those instincts were and how my life would manifest from there on. Fortunately I didn't listen to people who said I must be mad, because deep down inside I just knew it was right.

I became unemployed but strangely enough I didn't care about that either. Getting my emotional life back on track was much more important.

Out of the blue, two months later, I was asked to go back for a contract period of six months, with a good salary. This was great because the financial pressure was taken off — but then of course that contract came to an end. So, with some money in the bank, I just sat down one day at my computer and I started to pour out my heart into writing my letter. It seemed a very natural time to explain to my children what I was going through, and I was also experiencing this wonderful spiritual journey which I could not tell them about face to face.

My fingers flowed across the keyboard, sometimes till late at night — but I had no idea then that it would turn into a book, let alone help so many people. I remembered choosing the words *Before I Get Old and Wrinkly* at the time of my parents' death, little knowing that nine years later this would be the title for my book. To my children I may be seem to be getting old and wrinkly already but inside, whatever age you are, you never *feel* old!

When I decided to turn my letter into a book, the thoughts I put out to the Universe to help me with this came back to me in abundance. I was about to step far outside my comfort zone but deep inside I just knew it was right. Nearly all my friends thought it was a great idea. No-one said I was mad or *What if it fails?*

Suddenly magical things began to happen. A friend put me in touch with a publishing agent/coach who helped me make the decision to publish the book myself as this gave me more control. Then I met someone who introduced me to Authorhouse publishers, who were fantastic to work with. I didn't have the months or years of struggle and rejections that so many people do.

Then my friend Julie, with whom I had worked at her Mind Body Soul exhibition, offered to give me a free stand to launch my book. This fantastic opportunity gave me focus. But there was a catch — I had to give a talk at the exhibition.

Then a friend, Lesley Greenwood, with whom I had worked years before, offered to edit it for me. Another friend helped with the cover design. And after much soul searching, hard work and long sleepless nights, one day the book landed in my hands — an ecstatic moment. All the hard work had suddenly turned into a real, tangible thing.

My next challenge was the marketing: how was anyone going to know about my book unless I shouted to the world that I had achieved something which I hoped would help many people?

So, I did three things.

Firstly, I concentrated on getting the free stand displayed nicely. With the help of a friend, Theresa, I dressed the walls and tables with pink and black cloth to match the book cover. I blew up huge copies of the cover and laminated them into posters. I then had magnetic bookmarks made up as promotional business cards to give away (these were a huge success) and promoted myself very strongly in the exhibition programme which was going out to more than 20,000 people before the event, as well as to people attending on the day. Then I went out and bought myself some pink and black clothes to wear.

Secondly, I wrote some powerful sales letters and a press release. This was a new thing to me, and I wasn't sure they would work, so I was cautious and only sent out eight to local companies.

The third thing I did was a lot of praying, mediations and visualisations. I visualised myself standing at the display, signing copies of my book, smiling and laughing with people; then I visualised myself standing in a seminar room giving my talk. I didn't concentrate on how many people I would sell or speak to, feeling content to leave that to the Universe.

And the Universe came up trumps, as my book launch exceeded my wildest dreams.

I sold and signed more than 100 copies — and this was only my first event. At my talk, it was standing room only; there were approximately 150 people in the room and they had to turn people away! The applause and the overwhelmingly positive feedback propelled me outside in floods of tears; my nerves had kicked in.

Still, people flooded to my stand, asking for more details, wanting me to give a talk to their group or company. I landed a big contract with a Matron's Trust within the NHS, and was asked to give a talk and run a workshop for its managers. I was blown away, as a whole new life was opening up for me. One thing I learned — and which is a valuable lesson at any time — is, *you never know who is going to be in the audience*!

But it didn't end there. Unbelievably, the sales letters and press release that I sent out the following Friday resulted in the phone ringing on Monday morning. On the end of the phone was a charming lady called Liz Mullen, who casually explained that she hosts an afternoon radio show called Tea with Liz on my local BBC Radio station; would I be free to come in on Friday at 3pm to have a chat to a few thousand listeners? I couldn't take this in, and started to run around the house shouting with joy. Then the phone rang again: the local newspaper wanted to do a piece on me. And so it went on.

I couldn't have asked for a kinder presenter for my very first radio interview. Liz made me feel completely at ease and I enjoyed every minute of the experience. A cup of tea was given to me during the programme — but I found my right hand shaking so badly that I decided to leave it until after the interview was over. (I can't feel it happening, but for some reason my right hand often shakes a little — so nowadays I take a plastic bottle of water with me when I give talks, rather than a glass!)

My eight press releases brought me a fantastic opportunity to promote my book but there was one more thing I had to do: my first book signing. So, I walked into my local Ottakars bookshop and asked them outright. And they said yes, just like that! Once I had done one book signing with them it felt natural to pick up the phone to all the other bookshop managers and say: 'I recently did a book signing at your branch in Chelmsford…' and of course with all that ready-made credability they could do nothing but say *yes* too!

I have to mention here that Ottakars went out of their way to accommodate me, and the people who worked there were wonderful to work with. Most of the branches did the publicity for me, and were genuinely interested in me as a person. It saddened me when they were taken over by a larger book chain, as I feel that that personal touch has now gone from some branches.

A couple of weeks later, my publisher Authorhouse asked me to give a talk on marketing at a seminar they were running for new authors, because of the success I was having. I managed to get a free ticket for a friend, Peter, who had written a book but had hidden it in a drawer; I thought this might inspire him.

The first presenter at the seminar had been flown over from America — and I have to say it was one of the most boring speeches the audience had ever heard: she simply read out her PowerPoint presentations. (That was my second big lesson in public speaking!) So when it was my turn to stand up and speak, my bubbly enthusiasm for the success I was having went down brilliantly.

I was then handed a business card by a lady sitting in the audience with the words: 'You have to join the Professional Speakers Association as that was fantastic!' Her name was Lesley Morrissey, and as we chatted I found out that she was a professional speaker and that she lives near me. So, we travelled home on the train together and have been firm friends ever since.

Peter also won the prize draw, to have his book published free of charge — so it was an eventful evening — and his book too is now in print. Having given my speech for free, the Universe rewarded me by giving my friend his gift.

Within a few weeks of the launch of my book, through visualisation, meditations and a request to the Universe for help, my whole life was about to change.

Visualisation exercise

> Visualisation is a powerful tool which you can use for anything you want to bring to fruition. A brilliant thing to remember is, *When you visualise, you materialise.*
>
> Imagine yourself in any situation that you want to take place. Maybe you want to open a business, attract a new partner or generally just

be happier. You may want to visualise yourself being healthy and slim, having a new car or even winning a race.

Shut your eyes and sit still for a little while as you let your thoughts become focused. Imagine yourself being in the situation you want, achieving whatever it is. Imagine the gradual steps you will need to take to make this happen. Imagine how you will feel, what you will be wearing, who you will be talking to, who will be with you as your success becomes real. See if you can see any colours associated with it and imagine that colour surrounding the situation or object. Make it as real as possible.

Example: You want a new house. Imagine sitting at a table, playing in the garden with your kids, walking around the house — even though you do not know this house yet. Read the property pages, visit local Estate Agents — anything to do with moving — but don't just visualise it, do it.

Visualisation is the most effective language in which an athlete can communicate with himself.

Athletes imagine every step they need to take to win. They play the scene over and over in their minds, always culminating in winning. A good example is Tiger Woods, who has always been totally focused. Many sports people believe that is how they too will reach their own success.

You may not be able to create a mental picture at first; don't worry about it. Many people find it helpful to practise by visualising something familiar like a special room in your house or your favourite restaurant. Imagine yourself being there, what the place looks like, the smells, the sounds ... scan the whole room in your imagination.

Make a point of visualising this every day. Keep doing it. You may like to have a few words to associate with your thoughts. An affirmation of your choosing can help keep your mind focused; saying something over and over again brings it more into reality.

Some people say that visualisation and meditation are the same thing; they are not. When you do a meditation you can visualise what you want — but you don't need to do a meditation to visualise anything. But you do need to do this every day or as often as you can. Remember those words at the beginning: *What you visualise you materialise.*

Keep focused, visualise the end result that you want, and you may be pleasantly surprised with the end result — as I was.

Now I am going to say something strange.

I have just said that you have to visualise what you want to happen, including all the little details of the end result. But it's important, also, to let the scene unfold naturally. This can be hard to do, particularly when you want a thing so badly — but you have to detach yourself from the end result and just let it happen.

Trust the Universe to take care of it, and know deep down that it will happen. When you try to control everything yourself, sometimes you can miss some unexpected opportunities that are presented to you. Synchronicity will begin to flow so watch, and notice, by each step you take, how things begin to unfold. See how the jigsaw pieces suddenly fall into place.

Gut instinct, hunches, impulses and intuition

The power of my mind was not the only thing that played a role in my success. The Power of Intention, The Law of Attraction, The Law of Creation and many other spiritual divine laws which I will list further on in the book all played their part. I kept my focus on my *intention* to make this a success. I *drew* people to me who could help so I created my own success through the power of my intention, feelings and thoughts. I also *detached* myself from the end result — which, as I mentioned, went way beyond my expectations.

It was also part of the grand picture that my spiritual guides and helpers wanted for me and my life's blueprint. By following my instinct to leave my job, I had followed my inner wisdom. It was as if a wise person had gone ahead of me, seen the future, and come back to tell me which way to go and what to do. That wise person had seen the bigger picture of my life — the Grand Design, you could call it. But what turns out to be the right path does not always lie where you think you should be going! (See Chapter Six.)

Gut instincts are like messages from your mind and Higher Self; you just know that something is right — or that something is wrong, as the case may be. There have been many reported incidents when people *just knew* not to get on a train or plane which later crashed. And I am sure we have all had that feeling, at some time, that we needed to call someone just when that person has had a real need and was grateful for the call.

Instincts are like emotions you cannot create for yourself. When your heart starts fluttering, or your stomach may churn, these are emotions that just happen. You did nothing to make them happen.

In fact, sometimes you *have* made them happen. You might have bumped into the love of your life, you may have seen something that frightened you, or something unexpected could have taken you by surprise. When the heart flutters, this is something that you, yourself, cannot control. It is an expression of an emotion.

Tears are another emotion that you often cannot control. If something upsets you, tears may flow. You might see or hear something beautiful that reduces you to tears, which just appear. Gut instincts are like that too.

You need to follow your instincts, hunches and feelings about things, rather than ignore them. You do pay attention to the heart-flutter and the tears — so why don't you take more notice of other feelings, and thoughts which may suddenly pop into your head? Perhaps if you learn that these are an inner guidance system giving you warnings or advice about your way forward, you can begin to learn to trust them more. They are connected to your mind and your Higher Self — which is the higher, wise part of you.

Gut instinct and intuition are also how your spiritual helpers get messages to you. They come into and from the soul, your inner and Higher Self. One of the most important things to learn is how to recognise and follow your intuition — the little messages that pop into the head or a vision you might see or feel. Everyone *has* intuition but generally people don't know how to differentiate between their own thoughts and feelings, and intuition.

Your spiritual helpers also contact you through your dreams. It is worth noting down a strong significant dream or vision when you have one. These are indicators of your way forward, or of your fears.

When you write down a dream, try to analyse what your feelings and thoughts are about the dream's meaning. Dreams are powerful and there are many dream interpretation books which can help you understand their meanings. These can guide you to a general overall meaning, which you then have to personalise in order to make sense of what the dream is telling you by connecting all the parts together.

You also have to learn how to take the rational mind and the ego out of the equation. This is hard because you often think you know best when analysing your own thoughts. It does not require hours in meditation to pick up the thoughts from an intuition — all you need is a stillness of your mind at any time of the day. It is a knack worth learning.

Surprisingly, when you follow your intuition it leads you to freedom.

The mystery of your mind

My life was beginning to change beyond anything I could have imagined. I started to take each day as it came, visualising what I wanted and sending thoughts out to the Universe.

But I also want to mention here that you have to *feel* your desires and emotions, so that they can be attached. Just sending positive thoughts out to the Universe does not work. When you understand how powerful your thoughts can be, you can set your goals higher and create your own success in whatever area you wish.

Thoughts are the voices in our heads. When you are consciously aware — when you take the time to think about how and what you think — you wake up to the reality of how powerful they and you are. You can change your whole life by becoming an observer of the voice in your head.

Thoughts are not wispy little clouds or bubbles drifting through our heads. Scientists call them *measurable units of energy*. Thoughts are biochemical electrical impulses — cosmic waves. These waves of energy, as far as scientists can determine, penetrate all time and space.

Everything you see, hear, touch, taste and smell, including things you have not yet perceived, is made of energy. Each has a different vibration but everything is interconnected and abundant. We as humans are energy transmitters and receivers. Plants and animals have a lower vibrational energy but function the same.

For example, an acorn starts off very small and automatically grows taller and higher into a tree, as it raises its vibration towards the Universe when it is fed and watered. In the same way a small thought, repeated often to ourselves, can grow into something much bigger.

The thoughts you think today, the feelings you feel today, and the actions you take today will determine your experiences tomorrow and further in the future.

It is very similar to the saying, *What comes around goes around.* Just imagine your own thoughts coming back to you like a boomerang. The strange thing is that, by the time they do return, you may have forgotten that you sent them out in the first place, and wonder why something has happened!

Thoughts affect our bodies as well as what happens to us in life. For example, experts know from a polygraph or lie detector test that the body reacts to a person's thoughts. They change the heart rate, blood pressure, breathing rate, muscle tension and even temperature.

They also send out an energy vibration, and attract more experiences of the same vibration. So, a positive thought will make you feel energised, more centred and alert. They stimulate endorphins in the brain which create excitement and pleasure.

Attaching emotions to our thought request strengthens the energy signal you send out. This is important: thoughts *without feelings and emotions* take longer to bring to fruition.

Friends are also connected in a vibrational way. You attract friends with the same vibrational energy as yourself. *Like attracts like* is not a cliché; it's a truth. Friends are on the same wavelength, which is why the same people often form groups or clusters with individuals who are similar to themselves. When your vibration is raised to a new level you may find that some of your old friends, who are not aligned to the person you are becoming, will gradually drift away. That is because your energy and theirs are no longer on the same wavelength or vibration.

You can also be repelled by someone as soon as you meet them. You pick up their energy, which may not be aligned to your own, hence your distrust or instant gut reaction against them.

In Chapter Two I gave an example of your thoughts being like a radio signal. You can also think of your thoughts as a car navigational system. We all know that up in space there are satellites which pick up these signals. Imagine for a moment that you know where you are now, perhaps at home or in the office, you know where you want to get to, so you enter your destination into the machine. You are going from A to Z. The navigation system then tells you the best way to get there. It gives you specific directions, it never asks questions. It doesn't put doubts into your head while it gives you the clear message.

There may be a road blockage along the way; you go past but it has taken a little longer than planned to reach your destination. Alternatively, at the road blockage you could turn round and go back home — but you would have to start all over again if your journey is important.

These radio and car navigational signals are just like your thoughts. They go out to the Universe, so what you are saying to yourself you will reap. The good positive thoughts as well as the negative toxic thoughts are far more powerful than anyone realised years ago.

> *It has been proven now scientifically that an affirmative thought is hundreds of times more powerful than a negative thought.*
> *— Michael Bernard Beckwith*

But you must be completely clear about exactly what you want. The Universe cannot respond if you send out mixed messages. 'Well *that's* easy,' I can hear you say. Everyone knows what they want — don't they?

In fact that's not true. Many people haven't got a clue or perhaps only have vague ideas about what they want, so their information is not clear and precise. Imagine trying to tune into a radio station with a weak signal; you just get crackle. That's what the Universe often hears! You have to focus your thoughts but attach the emotion to them too. This will strengthen your request.

In Chapter Two we discussed the words like 'can't', 'but', 'if only' and so on … remember to take those negative words out of your vocabulary.

A mixed message is something like this:
- I want to be well as I don't want to be sick or feel ill.
  (It started positive but had a negative ending.)

- I want to have financial security as I don't want to experience the lack of money.

- I can't find a perfect man as they are all gay or married. (You *will* meet a lot of those men because they were included in your thought!)

Turn those sentences around like this:

- I want to be well as I would love to get back to the gym and take long walks with my family.
- I want to have financial security as it will enable me to do lovely things and go on holidays to places I want to visit.
- I want to attract a partner who shares my values and will help me reach my goals.

Turn the negative reason into a positive reason and you change your thoughts.

Another analogy is to imagine that you have been given a secret telephone number to the Universe, enabling you to talk to the infinite higher powers whenever you wish. In fact, you have that secret number already: your thoughts and your heart's desires. The higher infinite powers are always listening to your telephone call — but you can prevent the telephone line from crackling by making your communication clear and precise.

When you are clear and precise, your answers start coming back to you in your thoughts and in other ways such as synchronicity. The best time for ideas to pop into your head is through meditation — but you can talk on your secret telephone line any time you like, when you are quiet. It could be in the car, on a train, sitting or going for a walk.

Sometimes a book may jump off a shelf and give you answers you seek; you may bump into someone who can help. Your prayers, your thoughts and your ideas are always answered but not always in the way you expect!

Something To Think About

- Make up your own sentences and turn the ending around.

- Remember some of the things you have been saying to yourself recently. Are you sending mixed messages?

- Set aside five minutes. Sit in your chair and reflect deeply on what you have just read.

- When you become consciously aware and begin genuinely to notice your thoughts, you change the outcome.

My conscious thoughts start to amaze me

Going to see Randy Gage speak at the Yes Group meeting brought home to me how powerful our thoughts can be.

My 'Bridget Jones' relationship with Graham had come to an end after four years. He was ten years younger than me and he wanted children, which at my age was not an option. I hadn't seen him in years — yet, over the prior month, I suddenly started wondering about him and whether the children he had so desperately wanted were now in his life. It would have been sad if he were still single, as he was a lovely caring person but also a very powerful business man; would they have changed his life, I wondered.

I came away buzzing from Randy's talk, inspired by his message that you can change our own life through your thoughts. It was confirmation of what I had always believed.

It was 11pm when I jumped on the underground train, to catch a connection to my train home from the main line station. I settled into my seat, put my bags next to me — and looked up to see Graham a few feet away, smiling and laughing as he spotted me too. Of all the people to bump into that night, after six years! The other passengers must have thought I was mad, when I suddenly burst out laughing.

He sat down opposite me and we laughed and chatted all the way home. Sadly, he doesn't have children but does have a fantastic new job based in London, travelling all over the world. So when he asked me how things were in *my* life, I laughed out loud.

I told him that I had written a book and that he was in it! His expression was a picture. I also said that I now give motivational talks and that they occasionally included some of our experiences. All too soon, the train arrived at Graham's station so I never actually told him which ones I talk about — but they are the fun synchronicity experiences that I have mentioned before, and a brilliantly sexy one which I will mention in Chapter Five.

Meeting Graham on the train like that, after all those years, brought it thundering home to me that our thoughts are incredibly powerful. I also know that the Universe let it happen so that I could share this with you in this book, and in my talks.

What I had done is called *allowing*. When you *allow*, you are letting go of the results and trusting that whatever comes will be just fine. In my case this came back to me in a special and unexpected way; when you *allow* you cannot fail to create whatever you want. But you do have to be open and free inside yourself, to allow this to happen — which means overcoming the limitations inherent in your ideas of what should be or how things should happen.

Do you remember we talked about this earlier, when I mentioned that you have to *detach yourself* from the end result? Don't try to control it. Trust that it will happen and it will.

Your conscious and subconscious mind

Inside your mind and heart lies your success. Your soul and subconscious mind act like a computer: the soul stores everything that has happened to you in your many lifetimes. (Nearly all of us have been on this planet before, some of us many times, and many of us will come back again too! There is more about this in Chapter Eight.)

Most of us have some awareness of our conscious thoughts — but it is important to become aware of your *sub*conscious thoughts as well. Your subconscious mind is your lifetime's computer and is pretty much running the show. Since most of us have a negative tape constantly playing in our heads, we are continually sending out negative messages. You must learn to reprogram your subconscious mind, so that you can transform your negative self-talk and thoughts into healthy positive ones.

Unfortunately, many of us have a stubborn tendency to hold on to our old negative thoughts and self images. It's your comfort zone; you've become accustomed to your familiar concepts of reality, and you get stuck in our subconscious beliefs of fear and doubt. Most of these limiting thoughts and feelings stem from the past incidents, beliefs, and experiences that we talked about in Chapter Two; we have turned them into our personal truths.

You must be willing to release your negative mental programming, and step out of your comfort zone, to make room for a positive belief-system. Beliefs are just our habitual thoughts, and they can be changed through affirmations, self-talk, behavioural changes and visualisation techniques. I cover each of these powerful techniques within this book.

Because negative programming can be so deeply rooted, if you experience great difficulty in letting go, I suggest that you explore other techniques which may help.

Emotional Freedom Technique (EFT) is a powerful tool, as is The Sedona Method which you can find at www.sedonamethod.com. Even more tools can be found on the Internet or by visiting a library or bookshop. You may like to read Eckhart Tolle's book, *A New Earth: Awakening to Your True Life's Purpose*, in which he talks about the *ego*, which is directly connected to your thinking.

The conscious mind

The conscious mind is the part of you that thinks and reasons, that you use to make everyday decisions.

Your free will lies here, and with your conscious mind you can decide exactly what you want to create in your life. You can also accept or reject any idea in this part of your mind. No person or circumstance can force you to think consciously about what you do not choose. The thoughts you do choose will eventually determine the course of your life.

With practice, and a little bit of discipline, you can learn to direct your thoughts to only those that will support your chosen dreams and goals. Your conscious mind is powerful — but it is the more limited part of your mind. It includes your short term memory, which itself is limited.

The subconscious mind

The subconscious mind is far more spectacular. It is often referred to as your *spiritual* or *universal* mind, and it knows no limits — except those that you consciously choose. Your self-image and habits live in your subconscious mind. It is connected to your Higher Self at a much greater level than your conscious mind. It is your connection to God, your connection to Source and to Universal Infinite Intelligence.

Some people say this is your third mind — your higher consciousness.

You can think of the *universal mind* as the combination of all existence, and even the mind of the divine. Thought is Man's connecting link with the universal mind, and this is how you can affect others through your thoughts.

The subconscious mind is timeless, and it works in the present tense only. It stores your past learning experiences and memories. The subconscious mind thinks literally, and it will accept every thought that your conscious mind chooses to think and put in there. It has no ability to reject concepts or ideas; it simply accepts and stores them. This means that you can choose to use your conscious mind deliberately to reprogram your subconscious beliefs, and your subconscious mind has to accept the new ideas and beliefs because it cannot reject them.

But you can actually make a conscious decision to change the content of your subconscious mind.

Desire must be impressed upon in your *subconscious* mind before it can be manifested. Desire that is merely conscious seldom gets you anything; it's like letting a daydream flash through your mind. The desire must be visualised, persisted and concentrated upon so that it is impressed into your subconscious mind.

The worst thing you can do is undo all the implanting by going out the next day and tearing it all up with doubts and fears. By being single minded you will channel the required energy for it to manifest into reality.

Affirmations

A good way to do this is to say an *affirmation* to yourself, over and over.

These are powerful communications which you send to your brain, in order to change your behaviour. Write them down, record them on your iPod and play them to yourself, again and again. They must have a meaning to you, as you feel the love and joy they will bring. If you don't really believe, deep down, that you deserve to receive it (or if you don't truly want it) it either won't happen at all or it will takes ages to materialise.

For example, if you say an affirmation for a new partner to come into your life but you don't feel you deserve one, then he or she will not manifest because you are sending mixed messages. Change your thoughts and say instead, *I am good enough, I love myself.* Believe in yourself, believe that it will happen, and it will.

An affirmation can be about anything you want to believe that you can change or achieve. Overcoming an illness, starting a new business or simply to bring positive ideas and feelings into your mind are all good examples. Many top people agree that their own affirmations helped change their life. Louise Hay was the pioneer in this thought process; she has helped millions of people to change their lives and has written many books on the subject.

As you start to do this, you can then watch the reality of events happening that you have chosen to submit to your subconscious mind. It is the Power of Intention that has such a powerful consequence. Dr Wayne W Dyer's book *The Power Of Intention* is well worth reading. Lynne McTaggart has also written a number of books on this subject including one called *The Intention Experiment*.

Self-talk always says 'you' should or shouldn't have done something. You are giving yourself thoughts which your conscious mind believes. We all have an *ego*, which is part of our make-up — but is your ego resonating with the person you want to be, or is it still reminding you of your old conditioning thoughts and guilt's? Your ego makes you feel special and is very powerful.

When you learn to raise your consciousness and begin to awaken to your soul's true calling, you will suddenly realise that no-one can ever claim you again. When the old patterns reappear in your life, you will be able to sit back and look upon them with amusement. They can never affect you as they used to, and your ego will gradually become less prominent and less important as you learn simply to *be*. You set yourself free because you go beyond your ego and into freedom.

By only using and being aware of your conscious mind, you are using only a fraction of your true potential. The conscious mind is much slower and only represents about one sixth of your full mental capacity!

Your subconscious mind can take you where you want to go, and help you reach your goals in life much sooner and more easily than your conscious mind ever could.

You also need to have your mind set clearly at what you want to achieve. You have thousands of thoughts every day, and sometimes you have to think about something specific over and over again until a clearer thought comes into your head.

Question your thoughts

You also need to question your thoughts, especially the darker ones. You *believe* your thoughts, so it is important to understand how to let those go. One good way of doing this is to ask yourself two questions relating to a negative thought:

1. How does this negative thought make me feel? How am I reacting to it?
2. Who would I be without that thought? How would I react differently if I realised how that thought is affecting me?

To take this thinking process further, you could read Bryon Katie's book *Love What Is*. She also runs a programme called *The Work* which may interest you.

You need to tap into the vast power of your subconscious mind and Higher Self in order to use it to your advantage — but how do you do that? Time spent quietly without any external distractions will strengthen your connection to who you really are. Your subconscious mind knows who you are, as it has been with you for so long and is part of your soul.

You can use various techniques including meditation, visualisations, affirmation, prayer and being still with your mind. Stillness of your mind is also one of the most powerful focus techniques you can use without doing a full meditation.

Stillness exercise

> A *stillness* will give you many answers. A wonderful way to start to still your mind, other than meditation, is to take a walk in Nature, just sit by a tree or a river and think of nothing. Be aware of the flowers, the birds, the calmness of your surroundings. Go deep inside yourself to feel the air that you breathe. Be in the stillness of the moment. Push your worries aside. Perhaps lie down on the grass and use your senses to feel the energy that surrounds you. Everything in Nature is made of energy too, and you are connected to it.
>
> At other times of the day, become more conscious at each moment of what you are doing. Be aware of everything you do, whether you're sitting in a chair or concentrating on your feet and your steps as you walk. Washing your hands, feel the soap and the water as you wash.
>
> Be in the moment. Let it be as if you are sitting back and watching yourself perform these tasks; you are an observer, so you become consciously aware of the present moment. Trust your impulses. Be in the stillness of the moment and the stillness within you.

Studies have been undertaken with American soldiers who had become addicted to highly addictive drugs, such as heroin or opium, which they had taken in a war zone. When the soldiers returned home they often either no longer took them or didn't need to come off them with Methadone. Merely changing their environment enabled them to break the habit. Yet, when they returned to the war zone, they often began to take the drugs again.

What was going on? Was the power of their minds strong enough to overcome the addiction? Did they not need the drugs at home because they were surrounded by friends and family there? This is an interesting study, not yet concluded, which shows how powerful your mind can be.

Connection to your heart

Positive thinking is all very well, and you can learn how the process works. But if your desires are not genuinely coming from your heart, why would you want to create something not aligned to your truest self? Your core being knows deep down whether you are being honest with yourself: you cannot fool it!

Sometimes you think that if you have a particular thing in our life — a bigger house, a faster car, a fantastic bank balance — then this will be the answer to making you happy. Yet, how many times has this happened and you are still left feeling empty? You then move on to wanting something more or different, expecting *that* to give you the feeling of happiness. 'Neediness' is not a good place to be.

When you create via your thoughts sent out to the Universe, and when these thoughts are aligned to your heart, your emotions and feelings are automatically attached — and this is much more powerful than you can imagine.

Many scientists now believe, and are starting to prove, that our heart and thoughts are connected; the heart can create on its own because of the passion that is attached to the feelings of acquiring or achieving something. The Institute of HeartMath Research Centre in America (which is one of many) has been doing research into the heart and mind connection and found that over 93 per cent of stimulus is directed from the heart, which creates your reality.

This makes sense: your heart is connected to every part of your body, including pain, stress, nervous and hormonal systems, which of course resonate in your brain. The interactions include your courage, strength and wisdom. You feel with your heart and think with your brain — but they are entwined.

Following your heart and *not* your brain can be very difficult. To follow your heart is the most beautiful thing you can do but can also be the scariest.

Where this is a life-changing experience, it can be easier to do if you live or work on your own, as you may not need to involve anyone else. When you have responsibilities to partners or family members it is harder to take chances in case they fail. And yet, even when your heart is screaming at you to do something, and you know you want to do it, you still don't always follow it through. This can be frustrating, and sometimes heartbreaking, because it can leave you with an emptiness deep inside. It does take courage but if you can follow through it can change your life and the lives of those around you.

My own story is a classic example. My heart was telling me to turn my letter into a book and because I was living alone it was much easier for me to do this. No-one was relying on me and if it failed (a possibility which didn't occur to me at the time) then I only had myself to worry about.

Another turning point for me was when I read a book by Esther and Jerry Hicks called *Ask and it is Given*. This is a channelled book containing the teachings of 'Abraham' on how to manifest your desires. 'Abraham' is a non-physical entity who speaks telepathically through Esther when she is in a deep meditative state, and offers 22 powerful processes to help you achieve your goals. Some find the book hard to understand but it is a very powerful teaching.

The book relates to your own thought process but also to your feelings and emotions. It includes several chapters explaining how important these are. My favourite is Process 12, which explains one of the best thoughts and words you can say to yourself, *Wouldn't it be nice if...?*

That sentence says you are choosing what you want, and that you are being soft and easy about it which is a much gentler vibration and thought.

The book also gave me clarity on what I was experiencing and my beliefs. I went to see Esther speak at St James's Church in Piccadilly in London, through their 'Alternatives' programme, where many top spiritual speakers talk on a Monday evening.

To speak at 'Alternatives' is one of my ambitions; I will do it one day although I don't think I am ready yet. Previous speakers include Dr Wayne W Dyer, Brandon Bays, Deepak Chopra, Eckhart Tolle, Doreen Virtue, Marianne Williamson and Susan Jeffers. All have written spiritual books which you may like to read at some stage.

Some time ago I also read a beautiful book by Gill Edwards called *Living Magically*. It contains a story I love which demonstrates how the way that you think and believe can be so inter-connected. It is also about our attitude, which in some ways is even more important than positive thinking! Here is an extract:

Let's imagine two people, Joy and Gloom, who visit London one weekend. The first visitor, Joy, experiences a wonder-land of historical sites, museums, parks, theatres, shops and entertainment — a city full of friendly, smiling and colourful people. Gloom, on the other hand, sees a noisy, grimy city with crowded underground stations, overpriced restaurants, jostling strangers and mournful faces. They visited the same city, perhaps the same places, and spent the same amount of money — but Joy had a marvellous time, while Gloom was thoroughly miserable from start to finish. Why?

The secret lies in their belief system. Joy holds the following beliefs: 'Cities are exciting places to be.' 'People are generally friendly and helpful.' 'Life is to be enjoyed to the full.' Gloom, in contrast, believes: 'Cities are horrible places to be.' 'People are usually unpleasant.' 'Life is a burden — but we all have to struggle on.' No wonder they experienced a different London.

Whilst standing in the same street Joy and Gloom noticed and brought forth into their life what they believed would be true through their thinking, reasoning and belief system.

Joy would be drawn towards the shops and restaurants which had friendly, helpful staff — while Gloom would bump into those who were stern and morose. Joy would happen across the unexpected delight of street theatre or a parade, while Gloom might attract muggers and crooked salespeople, or witness a street fight. Both would return home believing they were right: London really is a wonderful/terrible place! Our beliefs are not based upon our experiences, but vice versa. Our experiences are created by our beliefs.

Mind and body connection: your energy field

In this chapter, we see that our hearts are just as powerful as our thoughts in creating the life that we want.

But it is interesting that you cannot separate your mind from your soul or your body even if you want to. Your mind, thoughts and also your body is made up of energy which has far more in common with everything that surrounds you than you realise.

Everything is energy. Humans, animals, plants, the water you drink, the air you breathe and even the chair you sit on. This idea seemed far fetched to me at first, so I asked a friend Malcolm to explain it to me in plain English. Here is what he said:

'This is pure Physics; matter is made up of molecules regardless of the state it is in — whether it appears to be a solid, a liquid or a gas. If you look at what appears to be solid and unmovable (like a rock) under a powerful microscope, you'll discover that it is made up of molecules, and each molecule is made up of atoms — and they are moving constantly, spinning.

'The reason the rock doesn't disintegrate is because there are magnetic forces holding it together. There are electrons and protons in the atom that act like magnets, attracting and repelling.

'In a solid form the energy inside the molecules is enough to keep it together. As more energy is imported to it (like heat or electricity — such as radiation or even a laser) it changes its state to a liquid — a flowing solid; even a rock becomes lava under conditions or great heat. The core of the solid, now semi-liquid, has molecules moving so fast that they are moving apart, reduce the magnetic the attraction and this allows a more fluid state. At the edge of the substance some are moving so fast that they spin off as gas.

'So the chair you're sitting on is actually moving — and we're connected to everything we come into contact with.'

We are all connected, and we are all one huge energy field.

Science is now proving that what you think also affects other people all over the world through your thoughts.

Malcolm went on to say: 'Scientists know that the essential communication mechanism of the Universe is quantum frequency, connected by a giant matrix — the Zero Point Field. This is a vast, inexhaustible quantum energy, consisting of sub-atomic particles which pass energy back and forth like a ceaseless game of tennis or squash. All things (including us) are packets of pulsating energy and this quantum energy field is one vast information headquarters like a universal computer which is space or the Universe as we know it. The brain perceives the world through this quantum frequency, as do our cells and DNA.'

When I run workshops or give a talk, I often refer to the person each of us is as *a unique individual* (which you are) — but I have also accepted that we are each a tiny particle within the whole Universe. I don't mean by this that we're so small that we cannot be recognised. In fact, I mean the opposite: we are all individual people with our own unique quirks, thoughts, wants and desires.

When you can imagine yourself as an individual particle, connected to everything you come into contact with, I hope you can begin to realise that you are no better or worse than anything or anyone else living on this planet. You should not judge others, because what goes on in their minds is unique to them.

Science has moved forward significantly in the last few decades, and is beginning to understand more about how the Universe works. This is something that has been studied and mystified people for many years. The science aspect never used to interest me because of the experiences I'd had, and instead I appreciated how powerful and wonderful the Universe and its helpers can be. I did not understand how it all worked — and I still don't.

Some of my experiences have been so profound that there are hardly words to describe the feelings, or to explain what happened. They are terribly personal to me, and only I can feel, hear and see them. I suppose I could say that it is a divine pure love which cannot be explained – only felt and experienced.

But if I were tapping into something which is unreal, how would I 'feel' the tingles, 'see' my pictures and 'hear' these voices? Many people all over the world are experiencing something similar, so maybe one day science will progress even further when the scientists experience this in person for themselves!

The energy around you: your aura

I had an aura photograph taken about six years ago. It astonished me to see that we are all surrounded by energy and colour. When I realised that this beautiful picture was me, I simply glowed! In the picture, I was surrounded by gold, white, red, purple and a little green. Even more powerful was that I had a huge spiritual Orb on my throat. (You will learn more about this in Chapter Eight.)

The aura photograph is on my website www.sheilasteptoe.com.

Your whole body is surrounded by an aura, which changes colour as you change. Recently I had another aura photograph taken, and my aura is now more green, gold, white and purple.

Many people sense auras and some can see them. I'm delighted to say that I have recently begun to see coloured auras around people, and I love doing this. To do this, you have to 'see' behind and around a person or object and not look into the centre. The aura radiates out, about two inches off the skin. It is transparent and tends at times to fluctuate from side to side, or to enlarge itself.

Aura exercise

You will need the assistance of another person. Ask this person to stand in front of a plain wall with no patterns — preferably either white or black. Place yourself directly in front of them, about ten feet away or more.

Looking directly at the bridge of the person's nose, or just above in the centre of their forehead (their 'third eye' area) you will start to have peripheral vision — in other words, you will be able to see objects in the room without having to look directly at them.

Move your eyesight slightly up now, to the centre of the person's forehead. Remember, because the aura is transparent it cannot be seen directly. Now move your eyes up higher to behind and around the person — and this is where I found I could see coloured auras. You may just see something faint to begin with. The aura resembles heat coming off of a road or fumes from a gas tank but it has more consistency, is less wispy.

To see a colour takes much practice but it can be done. Don't strain your eyes as this will cause double vision or a blur.

You may like to practise this outdoors, in Nature. Do this exercise whilst concentrating on a plant or tree. You can also do this on yourself but it is not as effective. Lie down with a pillow under your head and lift your leg or hand and concentrate on seeing the aura around your own body.

We all sense auras, usually without realising it. For example, when you have stood close to a stranger, have you ever 'felt' their personality? This is sometimes referred to as the human atmosphere. You may have visited a married couple's house and inadvertently interrupted a row. They greet you with a smile and pretend nothing has happened but behind this façade you can feel the pressure like the moments before a thunderstorm. You are not only reading their body language — you are sensing the emotions from their auras and this is why you know something is wrong despite the pretence.

Your aura has many colours and moves with you. It changes colours with your moods, feelings and health, plus your mental and physical state. Each colour represents a different aspect of you, and they blend into each other. I have read so many different versions of what each colour means that I will not include any here because I am not yet sure who is correct.

Plants, trees, animals and humans all have auras. Objects such as stones and rocks also have auras but they do not change colour as ours do.

People have been able to see auras for hundreds of years. Some people believe that artists could see auras, and that this is why pictures of many advanced spiritual people such as Christ, Buddha and their immediate students were all painted with golden haloes around their heads.

Something To Think About

Often I like to picture a white light surrounding my body. Imagine it from your head to your toes. Scan your body with your mind's eye, so that the light starts to expand slightly. Stand up straight with your shoulders back, and then walk.

Swing your hips as you walk along. Imagine you are ten feet tall, glowing with a white light radiating from you. You will start to notice people smiling at you; they won't realise that they are picking up on your aura and your energy. This is useful if you are going into a meeting where you want to take control. Feel the *presence* of you. Imagine this white light often — it's fun to do. It makes you and whoever comes into contact with you smile.

Let's recap...

STEP 1 — Meditate every day and keep a diary.

STEP 2 — Let go of fears, core conditioning and resistance.

STEP 3 —Visualisation and your thought process are essential for growth.

Affirmations are powerful tools. You should learn to follow your gut instincts, hunches and sudden ideas. When a light bulb flashes in your head, there's always a good reason.

I hope that you are beginning to realise just how powerful you are. Not only are your thoughts powerful but *you* as a person are too.

Please remember: through your thoughts you can create anything you want but you can also attract things you *don't* want. Where your attention goes, your energy flows.

It's important to be precise, to send a clear message to the Universe through our mind, and take your ego out of the equation. You need to move on and not live in the past, with your negativity and thoughts that may have been implanted many years ago.

We are powerful connectors and transmitters. Our spiritual helpers in the Universe will bring forth all that you desire as you become aligned with the person you are meant to be. That is not always who you think you should be. Your name may be 'Sheila', like mine — but who is the person inside, away from your thoughts?

Let's find out.

A Light Bulb Moment

Chapter Four

Believing In Yourself

If you think you can or you think you can't — you're right!
— Henry Ford

How many of us at some time fall out of love with ourselves, or perhaps with life in general?

There are times when gloom or darkness causes you to lose sight of the light momentarily. But it's good to remember that the sun is always shining above the clouds. Things may not be going as you wish, so you begin a downward slope; or you want to achieve something, maybe a new business or relationship, but you don't have the confidence deep within your core being.

This happens to us all at one time or another. A business or career that you have been pursuing for years becomes a chore and you don't enjoy it as you used to. Starting something new never seems to get your focus and remains a wish. Or a life event occurs which you are not expecting, such as a relationship ending, and it derails you.

I know first-hand how this feels. When my husband Bob suddenly left me for another woman, his midlife crisis became my crisis, and my whole world collapsed. My parents had recently died and I could sink no lower. I simply couldn't see my way forward. All I could do was take each day one at a time, each week and month the same, until after a period of time I began to climb out of the hole that had sucked me in.

Shocked and heartbroken, I didn't know how I was going to manage. But, as I explained in Chapter One, my whole life was beginning to open up in a spiritual way which helped me keep faith in everything — including myself. Thankfully, my confidence as a person was undamaged; for many people the most devastating events can bring on a failure of self-belief. They question everything, including whether the whole thing was their own fault.

Why *do* we blame ourselves?

If only I had known then what I know now. It would have lessened the pain, to have understood that often things happen for a reason. You can't see that reason at the time … but I can now look back and understand that if Bob and I had stayed together I would not be doing the things I am doing now. Bob and the Universe gave me a kick up the backside which I hated at the time — and yet I can see how important it is to 'go with your flow'.

Yes, devastating things happen. But you must never let outside influences take away your belief about yourself. We all meet these stumbling blocks at some time in our lives — and they help us grow.

We also have what I call 'blip' days, when things just don't seem to be going right. As long as you don't let them override your thoughts, and you recognise that sometimes these days happen, then it is all right to stop and reflect; it's normal and a part of life.

Some people take these 'blip' days and turn them into weeks. Or they use them as excuses to give up trying. It is then very hard to climb back up.

We each have qualities and achievements which get overridden by the negative things in life. It's tempting at such times to concentrate on what you haven't got, instead of what you do have and what you have achieved.

How often do you remember all the things you have already achieved in your life so far? You can be unwilling to let your light shine. You'd prefer to remain distracted rather than take responsibility for your own life. It's as if you are blinded by darkness, instead of letting the sunshine in.

When you look in the mirror you see yourself reflected. It would seem silly, wouldn't it, to blame the mirror if you didn't like what you saw there.

You spend hours wondering why you have failed or why something has happened. Instead, if you ask, *What can I learn from this?* or, *What has this taught me?* you can look at the inside instead of just seeing the outside.

Putting affirmation to work

Talk to yourself in the mirror. Tell yourself how beautiful you are, every day. We are *all* beautiful, deep within ourselves — but it can be hard to accept. Remind yourself of all the wonderful things you have achieved since your childhood. It may be hard to do this at the start. However, it can become a powerful exercise over time.

You *can* talk to yourself about your fears — but if you do, ask yourself where they come from. Are they real? Talk to yourself about how you can overcome them, by working out a strategy. For example, if you've failed your driving test, it doesn't mean that *you are a failure*, as so many people say to themselves. You just failed at that one particular task — there's a difference.

There are times in your life when you need to sit back and reflect on what a particular incident has taught you. If you don't take stock, it may keep repeating itself time and again until you do take notice. Sometimes the Universe will stop you in your tracks, so you have to slow down and pay attention!

I learned a huge amount about myself and my capabilities after Bob left. Of course, it took me a while to understand why I was going through that pain — but now I am so grateful (for me but not for my children) that this happened. One of the most important lessons I learned was *forgiveness*. I forgave him mentally, physically and emotionally, and thankfully did not end up feeling bitter and twisted. I truly forgave him after the pain settled down, because it opened a new path which in some ways presented me with a different life.

That last part may seem hard to believe. However, forgiving Bob gave me freedom and in the time since then I have grown into myself. I am now 'me' and not somebody's attachment.

Looking back, perhaps I took a step backwards in my marriage when I was raising our children — and at the time I was happy to do that. But of course the children grew up and left home. Would I have been able to pursue a career I wanted? That was a small issue within my marriage: Bob never felt comfortable about me going back to work when the children were older, so that is something I will never know.

Our separation has allowed Bob to grow, too. He always loved animals; horses were his passion, which I'm afraid did not interest me at all. Now he breeds horses, so *his* life has changed and he feels fulfilled.

I can see now that our life together was about bringing children into this world — but our parting had been pre-planned long before we met. I have no hesitation in saying that our marriage was meant to be, and I regret nothing. I learned from our marriage and have now moved on, as he has. Bob and I are still good friends. The children were desperately hurt but they have learned their own lessons from it, too.

We each have a life plan even before we come into this world. You agree with your spiritual guides and Master helpers what you need to learn on this planet Earth, what your experiences will be, and even whom you will meet on your journey.

Have you ever experienced *déjà vu*? When you meet someone for the first time, and it feels as if you have known them before? Or have you ever looked into someone's eyes and either had a beautiful feeling or an uncomfortable sensation that ran through your body; you might have taken an instant dislike, or even a step backward. This is often because of your energy vibration, which we talked about in the previous chapter — but it can also be about someone you *have* met before, in a previous life.

Such people can be triggers for you to remember your life's plan, even though you are not consciously aware. Everyone comes into your life for a reason, a season or a lifetime; when you study this poem, I think this will make sense.

People come into your life for a reason

People come into your life for a reason, a season, or a lifetime. When you figure out which it is, you know exactly what to do.

When someone is in your life for a REASON, it is usually to meet a need you have expressed outwardly or inwardly. They have come to assist you through a difficulty, to provide you with guidance and support, to aid you physically, emotionally or spiritually.

They may seem like a godsend — which they are. They are there for the reason you need them to be. Then, without any wrongdoing on your part or at an inconvenient time, this person will say or do something to bring the relationship to an end. Sometimes they die. Sometimes they walk away. Sometimes they act up or out and force you to take a stand.

What you must realise is that once your need has been met, your desire fulfilled, their work is done. The prayer you sent up has been answered and it is then time for you and them to move on.

* * * *

When people come into your life for a SEASON, it is because your turn has come to share, grow or learn. They may bring you an experience of peace or make you laugh. They may teach you something you have never known or done. They usually give you an unbelievable amount of joy. Believe it! It is real! But only for a season.

* * * *

LIFETIME relationships teach you lifetime lessons: those things you must build upon in order to have a solid emotional foundation. Your job is to accept the lesson. Love the person or people in question (in the way that is right for them) and put what you have learned to use in all other relationships and areas of your life.

It is said that love is blind, but friendships are forever. Thank you for being part of my life.

Something To Think About

- Can you relate to feeling instantly compatible with someone you have met?

- Have they brought anything into your life or taught you something?
- Have they made you laugh in a way you had forgotten you could, and brought back childhood memories of just being silly for a while?
- Have you let friends drift out of your life because you have moved on and don't share the same interests?
- Have you learned that forgiveness is one of the most important lessons, and that it sets you free?

Spread your own wings to fly

Allowing someone who is in your life to lead their own journey can itself be a liberating experience. Often you try to control other people, or people try to control you. Sometimes you believe someone else knows best — but they are not *you*.

While Bob was deciding whether or not to come back, and I was feeling desperate, a wise counsellor told me that I needed to let him go and sort himself out, for him to be able to return of his own accord; which he did, briefly, twice. That has been a valuable lesson: the truth behind the saying 'let him have wings'.

You need to let family and friends fly, so they can grow and feel fulfilled without being controlled. They also need to let *you* fly your own wings — because otherwise people can smother you. You are part of each other's lives but you cannot live their lives for them. You can support and listen — and even your children are lent to you, so you can teach and guide them — but you have to let them experience their own joys and heartaches.

This can be difficult. This is because we each come into this world as an individual soul and we will leave this world as an individual soul — but hopefully a more enlightened soul.

Each experience you have ever had has led you to where you are now. You draw to yourself, consciously and unconsciously, everything you have in life — so you shouldn't blame others if you find yourself at a stage which is not to your liking. You have drawn that event into your life because of the thoughts that you've had, the conditioning which you may not yet have released, and that is why it is so important to unblock past issues. We talked about this in Chapter Two.

Happiness is not something anyone can give you … or take away from you. Happiness is a choice. There is a purpose, a plan and a reason for all things. What doesn't make sense yet will make sense. Your challenges are what they should be, your rewards are what they will be, and if you can keep your faith the best is yet to come.

Conditioning may be holding you back, and the struggles that you encounter have diminished your self-belief. You can change all that. It is important to realise that change can be a blessing. You may not know where you are going right now, or what lies ahead — but you must trust that it is for your benefit in the end. You begin to see that it is like clearing the dead wood. It can be an opportunity to awaken new resources within you, to reassess the important things in life, and help you reclaim your aliveness, direction and sparkle.

Change is inevitable; nothing stands still from moment to moment. When things are going well you want them to continue for ever. Realistically, of course, this doesn't happen. You may take a wrong turning, through believing that you want something, only for it to turn out not to be where you were meant to be at all.

If I had not trusted, and gone with my flow in writing my book, I wouldn't be where I am today. Had you asked me a few years ago what I would be doing today, I would never have dreamt in a million years that this would be my life.

Our lives are in constant transition. And yet in our fast-paced, youth-obsessed, competitive, 24/7 culture we have lost touch with the natural cycles and rhythms of life. Sadly, we have lost the ability to turn this process into something magical that gives us insight, guidance and ultimately the space to embrace new opportunities. We *fear* change as a bewildering or painful process. Yet, change can be a gift from the Universe.

Change can be an opportunity to learn and embrace new things. We are all made for success but it is up to the individual to aim for it. Everyone has setbacks in life; that's normal and part of living. It is up to you to learn from each event, trust that it is for your own good, and keep praising yourself for how far you have already come.

Many people, such as myself, end up on a path that years before they would never have dreamt could happen. It is such a liberating experience, I wish more people would have their *Aha!* moment, rather than assume that it only happens to others. Your carriage on a railway track may suddenly take you in a completely different direction; just ride in it when that happens and see where it takes you. It could be fun!

There is a famous quote from Marianne Williamson in her book *A Return to Love:*

'Our deepest fear is not that we are inadequate. Our deepest fear is that we are powerful beyond measure. It is our light, not our darkness that most frightens us. We ask ourselves, Who am I to be brilliant, gorgeous, talented, fabulous? Actually, who are you not to be? You are a child of God. Your playing small does not serve the world. There is nothing enlightened about shrinking so that other people won't feel insecure around you. We are all meant to shine, as children do. We were born to make manifest the glory of God that is within us. It's not just in some of us, it's in everyone. And as we let our own light shine, we unconsciously give other people permission to do the same. As we are liberated from our own fear, our presence automatically liberates others.'

Susan Jeffers has written a book called *Feel the Fear and Do It Anyway*, which is an example of overcoming what you think you cannot do. You can shine, and the fundamental core belief you need to have is a belief in yourself.

You need to 'feel your presence'; the essence of who you are. You need to want to be noticed and expand yourself to shine your glory. You are magnificent as you are right now. But you may have to step outside your comfort zone, to find the courage, determination and persistence to reach new heights.

For many of us, life can seem empty. No matter how much success you have, or how many loving people surround you, there still seems to be a void which you cannot fill with all your busy-ness. For many of us, until we find our meaning and purpose we will continue to feel empty.

But when you learn to shine and realise that you do make a difference, that you are needed and that you are important you will realise how wonderful this world can be. We each have a special role to play. As you gently appreciate all that you have, and who you are, life begins to unfold as you gain more meaning, confidence and purpose. Be proud to be you.

Embracing change exercise

> In one of your meditations or visualisations, imagine going through a gateway or archway. Feel yourself step into the expanse on the other side. Don't be afraid: sometimes when you take that *imaginary* step, your life can change in an instant. See what you want to see on the other side and step across. Choose to be happy. The unknown can be a freedom beyond your imagination.

I find that to continue my own growth it is important that I keep learning. My quest for knowledge takes me all over the place. Meeting like-minded people, reading books which interest me and attending courses to learn different techniques or knowledge, all helps me to step outside my comfort zone. It also keeps my belief in myself.

One of the first courses I went on was at a spiritual college very near where I live — the Arthur Findlay College, near Stansted. My tutor, Stella Upton, was adamant that my unique gift was teaching. I found that I could resonate with some new techniques she showed us — however; I decided that I was not cut out to be a medium.

It was lovely to be in a spiritual environment where I could learn so much and meet so many new like-minded people. People come from around the world to study at the college, as spirituality is often not a subject people can discuss openly in their own country.

I also went along to my first Toastmasters event, which a friend Constance runs locally. I was told that I could just sit in the audience and watch and learn. Suddenly, the Master of Ceremonies decided that I could do a five minute Table Topic talk, and handed me a little newspaper advertisement about flowers. It was a week after Valentine's Day, so I engaged the audience by asking the men what amusing thing they had done for their partners! Shame on them for some of their answers

— but I am pleased to say that I won Best Table Topic Award and have a certificate saying so displayed in my office.

Each step that you take outside your comfort zone helps you feel taller and helps you shine.

The importance of praise

Praise can be a powerful exercise. It boosts confidence, self esteem and self worth. I wish everyone on this planet would praise more often, even for silly little achievements. Praise should not be just for big events.

One mission in my new career is to raise awareness about praise. In my coaching practice I come across too many people who have never been praised in their entire life. This has a devastating effect. I find something to praise them for and the joy it brings is astounding.

I constantly praise my grandchildren, too. My family looks at me sometimes as though I am mad. But in childhood, praise should be given on a regular basis. How many of us when given praise feel embarrassed and say, *Oh, that was nothing*, instead of accepting it graciously and with thanks? You *earned* that praise so why feel embarrassed? Or, when someone gives you a compliment, do you giggle or blush? If you watch yourself carefully you may even spot yourself shuffling your feet as if you wanted to run away and hide!

Stop right there and just say, *Thank you. How kind of you to say so!* This can be hard to do but just try it.

Before we go any further in this chapter, please stop reading for a minute and praise or compliment someone who is near you right now. It won't cost you anything so what's stopping you? It will bring a smile to your face and pleasure to the recipient.

We are each born beautiful and as we are meant to be. We are all different, with different expectations and goals — but some people achieve so much, while others fear to attempt important things.

You enter this School of Planet Earth to achieve something unique to you. We are each given the tasks and gifts of life to achieve this — so where has the confidence in ourselves gone? Did it leave you in childhood, teenage years or even adulthood? The good news is that you can get it back if you want to.

Have you ever considered how your words and actions affect others? Words can have a lasting effect … so, how must other people feel if yours are all negative? What words do you tend to say to your children for example? (There is more about this at the end of the book.)

Praising and negative words have a completely opposite effect. You know deep down that this statement is true — but how often do you stop and think before you speak?

Develop the habit of treating the words you say as important speeches. Take a few seconds to construct the speech in your mind. This may also be a good time to say *Sorry* or *Thank you* to someone, which can be hard to do. Or, *I love you*, because people can't read your mind! These few words can mean so much — and in some ways you are praising yourself for taking the initiative

Believing in yourself is everybody's right. Does it really matter what the person next door thinks about you? They have no idea about the person inside of you. *You* know who you are and *you* know your qualities — but shouting about yourself often goes against the grain of your conditioning. Your fear of other people's judgment overrides your confidence.

Like anyone else, there are times when I too have doubted or questioned the *should or could*s that kept popping into my head — such as the time I was paralysed by fear of my lack of qualifications — but when I know deep down that doing something is right, I am happy to step outside my comfort zone.

Believe it or not it can be fun! Writing my first book, and then this one, certainly made me challenge myself in ways I never dreamed of. Giving my first talk at the Mind Body Soul exhibition led me into an unknown territory — but I always trusted that it was the right thing to do, and more importantly that I could do it. Looking back, I'm glad I did because that very first talk led to other challenges that I wasn't expecting, and was also the start of a new career.

At the exhibition was a Matron from a NHS Trust in the Midlands, who asked me to give a talk and workshop for her managers. Another couple, Mike and Gill asked me to write for a new magazine, *Healthy Life — Mind Body and Soul*, which they were about to launch. I was also asked to give presentations to a number of companies, which was the start of my new business. All of these opportunities sprang from the launch of my book and a belief in myself.

My fear kicked in again: the NHS contract was a daunting event. But I rose to the challenge and when I actually arrived at the venue and saw all the lovely people and the room, my fears subsided.

When my new found friend Lesley Morrissey took me to my very first Professional Speakers Association event I was in awe. One of the first speakers I heard was a guy called Nigel Risner, a very successful speaker; I wondered what I was doing there, listening to someone who travels all over the world giving talks and earning a fortune. *This is out of my league*, I thought. But then someone said to me: 'He started one day just like you. He was once where you are now!' And they were right.

We all have to start somewhere, if we want to get anywhere! But you have to believe in yourself and your project or desires. I believed in myself and my new book so much that a year later I was on ITV's *This Morning* show (see Chapter Seven).

You can accomplish anything if you really want to.

My new business

I was beginning to love this new life that was opening up. In all my previous jobs I had been involved in Sales, working for someone else. However, I had been self-employed whilst working for BUPA, so the idea of focusing on what I wanted to do whilst working from home was not new to me.

Setting up a completely new venture was daunting. I wanted to take all these new experiences and turn them into something which resonated with me. But … how?

Each little step I took led me onto the next stage, and it all began to flow. I wanted to continue giving talks, which has become a passion, but I also wanted to run workshops to help people. How was I going to get people to come to them? What was I going to teach?

It started with two things.

I decided with a friend Theresa that we would work together. We'd not only create workshops, we would help others to do the same. Theresa's brother, an actor, wanted help to organise children's drama workshops so we set up a company called aspirations4u. I would run the workshops whilst Theresa took care of the business structure and accounts — each of us playing to our strengths.

Then suddenly her husband died, having been apparently healthy and aged only 39. However, all three of us had discussed the idea for our new company and he had been one hundred per cent behind it, so we somehow kept going. In fact, I now think this helped Theresa to stay sane, because it kept her mind occupied. She came with me to many exhibitions where I was promoting my book and giving my talks, so we were helping each other.

We both decided to attend a Business Link workshop on 'How to create a business plan'.

To my surprise, at the workshop I found the accounting side interesting. However, *my* job would be to set up a website to promote the business. The theme for our workshops was the importance of believing in yourself to create a better life — but I had no idea how to create a website to persuade people to sign up. One of Theresa's cousins came to the rescue.

Richard and I discussed what I wanted from this site. My main idea was to have a beautiful dove flying freely along with a workshop section, promotion for my talks and also my book. Richard set it up that I could add and change the wording with an easy-to-use system called Macromedia Contribute which I still use today.

But then Richard went to Australia, leaving me with the most frustrating time I have been through in years. He had control of the website, yet he was thousands of miles away falling in love and couldn't understand my growing irritation as the website suddenly wouldn't work. I was successfully promoting the website at exhibitions but no-one could get into it to register for our products.

The workshops came to a halt, my speaking business came to a halt and I had no sales from my book. All this taught me huge lessons! After five long months I found someone else who transferred the hosting to the company *he* used, and things got back on track.

But the sudden halt in giving talks and running workshops undermined my confidence and nerve again. The fear about my lack of paper qualifications kicked in and I had to fight mentally to conquer it and move forward.

The best way I found to do this was to concentrate on getting the content for my website and workshops into a better format — and the belief in myself did not wane completely. I was still giving talks at many Mind Body Soul exhibitions, and I ran one of my most successful workshops to date; delegates called it the most fabulous 'me' time workshop they had ever attended, so that I knew this new direction was the right one. I still wasn't earning a fortune but Fate was about to take a hand in my life again, as I kept my faith. (See Chapter Seven for more about goal setting.)

The spiritual side of my life was progressing but something else was happening too. That lapse of faith in myself prompted my spiritual helpers to give me another nudge, and they started to play around with me! Weird things started happening in my house as they strove to get my attention. I was so wrapped up in my new business that my focus on the spiritual had wavered.

An ashtray suddenly flipped about three turns off the side of my chair. The lights in my living room exploded and upstairs the shower kept turning itself on. I noticed that these events happened whenever I was thinking negatively. It was as if my guides and Angels were bringing themselves to my attention. At night time 'they' sometimes gave me a jolt and lifted my leg — exactly as if I were giving myself a kick up the backside. Sometimes 'they' tripped me up and I could feel myself fall; I realised that at that point I was heading in the wrong direction with my ideas.

Each event made me stop and reflect but I couldn't always understand what they were trying to tell me. *How* was I going down the wrong road? I'd thought that what I was doing was *right*! Gradually I began to realise that 'they' know best and were trying to help. I think they may have been feeling some of my frustration too.

Now that I have settled on my new way forward, these events haven't been happening — but they are powerful reminders that we can call on our guides and helpers, and they are always willing to give assistance when they can. They now give me assistance, if I stumble upon something which is right for me, by moving an object — but nothing so startling thank goodness. Knowing this gives me great confidence.

Our guides are never judgmental of us and our lives remain our own choice. We can have their assistance but we do need to ask. They will never impose themselves. They have a sense of humour, too.

You don't always follow your instincts, or an idea that pops into your head, but we all have guides and Angels that we can call on who give us support in our chosen life. (There is more about guides and Angels in Chapter Eight.)

Self-belief

Lack of self-belief can stem from when you compare yourself to others. Success means different things to different people. A small success can be just as worthwhile as something big. Other people may look up to you for your skills in an area which they admire but never have told you! Jealousy can also play a part here, too. We each have qualities, talents and unique gifts but we often hide them in case others think shining our own light is wrong. Avoid comparing yourself with other people; you don't have enough information to do it fairly!

Sometimes you need courage, determination and the sheer will to become the person you were meant to be. Don't squash those beautiful inside qualities. You were given them before you were born, along with your personality. During your lifetime, many people have helped to shape the person you are now — but others may have squashed you down, leading you to doubt yourself.

Believing in yourself is not always easy. However, when you have unconditional acceptance of the person you are — warts and all — you become much more powerful as a person. The following exercise will reveal your own strengths and weaknesses. Playing with your strengths enables you to have a belief in yourself which you should use to your advantage. It will also help you to value yourself and radiate your best qualities, which will help with self confidence.

Qualities exercise

Beside each word score: 0 = Almost never   1 = Sometimes   2 = Often   3 = Nearly always

(There are no right or wrong answers and no score, so be honest with yourself.)

Tolerant	Proud
Adventurous	Loveable
Cynical	Interesting
Intelligent	Shy
Irritable	Joyful
Depressed	Amusing
Self-conscious	Self Critical
Critical of others	Powerful
Free	Caring
Worthless	Happy
Kind	Sensitive
Trustworthy	Indecisive
Demanding	Miserable
Lazy	Optimistic
Stupid	Self aware
Flexible	Confident
Embarrassed	Boring
Foolish	Controlled
Guilty	Capable
Intuitive	Spontaneous
Fun loving	Open
Cheerful	Giving
Active	Dreamer
Bored	Tearful
Punctual	Secretive
Content	Passionate
Ambitious	Gullible

> Do you notice a pattern with the numbers above? Do your qualities lie within one certain area, and is there another which you feel you may need to work on?
>
> These qualities above are yours. They are your core beliefs about yourself. You deserve a good self-image.
>
> Choose some of the words above, write six *positive* sentences which you think describe you. Write 'I am' somewhere in the sentence — such as 'My core belief is that I am…'
>
> Now describe your talents and skills, at least six of them.

Do you assume that, whenever you put yourself first, you're being selfish? Do you tend to do what you think other people expect of you, rather than what you want to do yourself? So many of us give up our lives and hearts' desires to satisfy and please others.

Women are especially prone to this in motherhood. We often have children and husbands whom we always put first. But you still need to be the core person — and your needs are just as important as everyone else's.

It may be that in childhood you entered training for a profession that your parents wanted for you, which was not of your own choosing. It can be hard to stand up to such pressure when you're young — but now is your chance to change profession and follow your heart.

How *do* you change limiting beliefs into positives?

Attitude is the key. Imagine a football team going out to play a game, believing they are not going to win! What would be the point of the game?

Someone with big non-limiting beliefs will achieve big non-limiting things. Someone with small beliefs will achieve small things. That, too, is acceptable because small things can lead to bigger things — it just takes longer. There is also the advantage of taking one small step, then another, until you reach the top of your ladder. Small steps are believable and therefore achievable.

Another way to challenge a limiting belief is to question its validity. When you question something enough, and gather contrary evidence, you begin to doubt it. Ask yourself, *In what way is my belief absurd? If I kept this belief, what would it cost me? What caused me to have this belief in the first place?*

By questioning your limiting beliefs you can develop an empowering belief about the situation or the thing you want.

You have to plant a seed in your own head first, for it to grow. For example, if you plant a bamboo seed, water it, tend it and look after it, nothing happens for six long years. And then suddenly it grows twenty feet in six weeks!

Passion and purpose

Nothing on this Earth is more powerful than passion and purpose. When you plant your seed to our purpose, passion ignites. Following your true calling in life — doing what you love — is the reason you are here. I believe that, underneath the surface, everyone has a seed waiting to grow. You need to water it and let the sunshine do the rest.

Unfortunately, many of us do not *know* what we want to do, so we just drift. It can be difficult if you don't feel a strong pull towards something. Even when you do, it can take a huge amount of courage, self-belief and a determination to succeed — but it is worth every single thought, every small step and all the hard work.

Everyone's passion and purpose will be different but we each have a unique role to play in this world. *Your* role might be based on a musical or artistic talent. You may have an affinity with children, or with flowers, or you might be a mechanical wizard. You may be drawn to certain political or social causes, or you may have a hobby such as pottery or gardening which you love. If you wake up every morning dreading the day ahead, you may well be in the wrong job. Do you spend all day itching to get home to play the piano? Then perhaps you should be doing something musical.

I wouldn't be where I am today if I had not followed my instincts, to follow an idea that had been planted in my head. At first, I felt I was deluding myself. I had never written an article, let alone a book!

But the idea wouldn't go away. Even though it scared me, I didn't *want* it to go away. I began to see the fun in doing something which would create a new me, and also give me more of a purpose. Today, I can't imagine myself ever retiring because I would hate to be without my lovely business which gives me such pride, passion and purpose. I like to keep pushing myself just that little bit further out of my comfort zone. When I succeed I am so delighted — even though I am scared while I'm doing it!

Do you hesitate to do something new out of a fear of upsetting others or of being ridiculed if it doesn't work? Imagine for a moment, going to your grave having never stretched yourself, and lying on your deathbed saying *If only*. Is that what you want?

Too many people are living other people's dreams or doing what they think is expected of them.

Something To Think About

- Do you wake up every morning with no enthusiasm?
- Do you find yourself sleeping all the time?
- Do you go to a job which you dislike, or have a relationship that doesn't thrill you any more — and are you frightened to make changes?
- Could you be going nowhere because you don't have a great destination to drive towards?

It's called a *purpose*. Once you find your purpose you will also discover more about how life can be. Things will magically start coming to you. New doors will open — but nothing will come your way without effort. Sometimes great sacrifice and even serious setbacks will come your way too. (We will cover this further in Chapter Seven.)

But your passion will override and drive you beyond your temporary pain. Your passion is a confidence and self belief builder. It's a career builder and a success maker. It's the greatest 'high' in the world as you begin to succeed.

Finding your passion and purpose is key — but it can be hard to find. Even taking up a hobby can ignite something as you get engrossed in it. Or your passion could be something very simple — because to be a successful entrepreneur is not for everyone, nor should it be.

To be a successful Mum or Dad is just as important. For example, Rose Kennedy, the mother of Robert F Kennedy (who went on to become President of the United States) and eight other children, said: 'I looked on child rearing not only as a work of love and duty but as a profession that was fully as interesting and challenging as any honorable profession in the world and one that demanded the best that I could bring to it.' She dedicated her life to her children because she knew that was her passion and the reason she was born.

Remember, you choose your parents — so each of Rose's children knew what she could teach them before they even came into her womb. (There is more on Passion and Purpose in Chapter Seven.)

Gaining more confidence

Confidence comes naturally to some people and is harder for others. But it can be the essence of personal success. People tend to forget about their own qualities and strengths. One of the most common ways to lack confidence is not feeling able to walk in a room ready to chat with everyone because you are scared; this happens to many people.

In contrast, being natural about yourself and having an air of inner self-belief is like walking around being ten feet tall.

Not everyone needs to like you or agree with everything you think and do. This may go against your conditioning but you need to give yourself permission to shine.

Occasionally you need to give yourself permission to fail — and also permission to succeed. You should stop worrying if people criticise you; they are not you.

We all have talents which stay hidden. You need to play to your strengths rather than comparing yourself with other people, who themselves have different qualities and strengths.

Let's consider a few questions:

- What scares you the most? What are your fears? What are you resisting?
- All children are born with confidence — when do you think you lost yours?

- What would make you get up every morning with joy? What excites you, that you could perhaps turn into a business or hobby?
- What thoughts won't leave you alone?
- Consider taking the following steps towards teaching yourself to act with confidence:
- Do something *a little bit* risky every day, which will bring you excitement. For example, pay a stranger a compliment.
- If you are shy, tell people and they will include you in their conversations. They won't misread your reserve as stand-offishness.
- If you would love to write for a living but think no one would read it, write one article.
- Take up a hobby or activity that would make you feel good.
- Lists your qualities and strengths. Ask friends or family for suggestions.
- Stamp out those negative thoughts, such as *you are unlovable* or *you can't…*
- Nothing has to be drastic. Take one small step, and then another. Taking a risk can seem daunting but successful people don't succeed without taking some sort of risk.

Daily habits exercise

> This exercise is about re-thinking your existing habits and routines. When you continue on a daily basis doing the things you always do, nothing else changes either. You need to break the pattern.
>
> Keep a diary of what you actually do each day. Are you doing the same thing over and over again? Does this bore you or thrill you? Do you do the same thing every week?
>
> Routines are good and provide a structure but is there time in between to do something different and exciting once in a while? Are you doing things out of habit or necessity?
>
> Aim towards one goal by changing a habit. Example: stop watching TV on a Friday night and go to a dance class instead. Make it a realistic goal because you will not achieve it unless you really can step outside your comfort zone.
>
> Keep a diary of all the scary little things you have done. When you do something that makes your heart pound, suddenly you realise you can achieve a little more.
>
> Accept that you might fail. And learn that in fact failure teaches you more than success does! You learn by your mistakes and they are *not* always failures. You are only a failure if you stop learning.
>
> Look your best. Dress up and feel proud.

- Confidence comes from your mind.
- Confidence comes from self-belief.
- Confidence comes from stepping outside your comfort zone.

A good way to gain in confidence is to hire a coach to help you step outside your comfort zone. A coach can help you come alive through a series of strategic steps — but please do take your time and find a coach that makes you feel inspired.

NLP training (Neuro-Linguistic Programming) is another good source of confidence building, especially in business. It helps you understand how the mind works and certain ways of getting your message across that can prove invaluable in business.

Many people, including coaches themselves, believe everyone should have someone to coach them to give them confidence, bounce around ideas and to give them encouragement.

If you can't afford a coach, ask a very good friend to help you. You would actually help each other in the process — and it could be fun.

We are not all confident people but we all *can* be. It takes time.

Body language

This subject fascinates me because the body sends out such a powerful message. It can say more than a thousand well-chosen words. You give an instant impression within the first minute or less — so it's crucial to get it right. A bad first impression can take ages to disappear so you need to be constantly aware of how you portray yourself to others and even to yourself.

Your body language can become a habit and you may be unaware of what it is saying. An open person is so much more relaxed and easy to talk to. Would you approach someone who frowns and has his arms tightly folded to symbolise a barrier and self-protection? He may be expressing the thought, *Don't come near me*, or he might be feeling guarded about what you might say to him. Of course, some people cross their arms because it is a comfortable position for them — so you would have to look beyond that and 'read' the rest of their body posture.

A person who is relaxed and at ease is approachable. Someone in love will look straight into the eyes of their lover, touch constantly and walk close to them as a gesture of friendship.

People may be 'touchy-feely' which can be uncomfortable for some but is often just a warm gesture. You need to look into people's eyes — it's not just a cliché that they are the windows of their soul. It shows you care and are interested in that person. Eyes are interesting because where someone looks also tells you about that person's thoughts. For example, when someone is looking down, they are normally 'feeling' their thought. When they look to the left they are 'visualising' that thought. When they look to the right they are accessing their 'memory' of that thought.

Nothing annoys me more than when someone I am talking to looks behind me. I could name a couple of people I have come across in business who do it constantly; they make me feel that they believe the person over the other side of the room can help them more than I can! How rude and self-centred that is. Of course, there are people who do this sort of thing because they are shy, feel intimidated or insecure but that is completely different; when you talk to them and show you're interested, they should gain in confidence and the habit will gradually subside as they begin to shine.

Body language is also about how you feel about your own body. Many people hide behind clothes — but many larger people who feel confident *ooze* charisma. They walk tall, stand straight and have style within their manner. Size does not matter but appearance does. Clothes do not need to be expensive and there are many programmes on television showing you how to dress for your shape; once you feel that you look good, you can go out into the big wide world and shout: *This is me!*

When you start to love yourself, others will love you too.

The true art of listening

'Active listening' is a skill which eludes many people. To really listen and hear what a person is saying is a fundamental skill everyone should learn. Many people miss words they hear because they are either thinking about something else or can't be bothered to concentrate. This is understandable when the conversation is boring — but in a true relationship you need to listen with depth. To hear is the most important part of any speech. To be heard is just as important.

In a two-way conversation, how often do you actually listen and show a real interest in the person as if you wanted to get into their soul? Asking closed questions (when the answer can only be a simple yes or no) gets you nowhere. Asking *open questions*, which encourage the other person to tell you more, begins the wonderful process of getting to know each other.

Of course there are times when it is inappropriate to ask personal questions. If someone wants you to know something either they will tell you straight away or you may need to dig deeper — but you must respect their wishes even if they never share intimate details. You are probably not the right person, or the time may not be right for them to open up.

In business it is important to understand what a person needs from you; when you actively listen you will hear. People often don't want to know what you can *do*, until after they have told you what they *need*. But if you are not truly listening, perhaps because you want to shout about what you can do for them, those words will just often go over their head! Their needs are far more important than yours.

The same is true in relationships with partners, friends, work colleagues and children. Do you truly listen to them? Do you take the time to stop and listen? That is one of the most important gifts you can give them. Your time is valuable but it is never more precious than when you give it to others. Giving time and listening is worth millions in the bank to them.

But how do you get people to listen to *you*?

First and foremost, when *you* start listening to other people, they become interested in *you*. You have shown you care and this begins to build a trust. Conversations need to be two-way; nobody wants to listen to someone always moaning and gossiping (unless they are a gossip themselves) or to someone who continually criticises other people. It's all too negative.

I admit that not every conversation can be amusing or even interesting — but all good conversations have an element of *interest*. People can get to know you by listening to your enthusiasm, your ideas and your knowledge. The key is in your voice.

Someone who has only one tone of voice becomes boring after a while. Have you noticed people who never express emotion in what they are saying? They ramble on and on and whoever they are talking to will switch off. It is important to make what you say sound fun by raising and lowering your voice as you speak. People will want to hear what you have to say.

You can practise this by recording yourself and then listening to how you sound. We all hate the sound of our own voice, so expect to have to override that feeling — and listen to the depth of what you are saying. Read aloud and listen to yourself when your voice goes into excitement. You could even video yourself and watch the body language too!

There are many people who are trained as a voice coach who could help.

Look for humour in your conversations and people begin to listen. If you find yourself in a conversation that's going nowhere, turn it around and take control. You don't need to shout but you do need people to listen to you because it makes you feel wanted, and helps you gain confidence. It gives you a true belief in yourself.

Listening exercise

Adopt the 2:1 rule. Listen twice as much as you talk. This is why you have two ears and only one mouth.

Ask someone an open question, or deliver a closing line if you are a salesperson, and then … … … don't say another word for *three whole minutes*. Sit and count to 180 seconds to keep your mind occupied but *don't butt in*. You are asking another question when you do that, so your first important question may not be answered!

When I worked in Sales, some of my colleagues found this very hard to do — but as a trained counsellor it was easy for me. It gives the other person breathing space, although it can make *you* feel uncomfortable — but it works wonders in both work and personal friendships.

What do you believe about yourself?

I have learned so much about myself and the Universe from the spiritual circle that I joined (see Chapter Eight). My spiritual experiences are still going on. I have a gift which some people say you have to be born with — but that concept is rubbish. I was in my mid-forties when it all started to happen, and as you read further you will discover that everyone can access this gift if they want to. You may need to ask your 'helpers' to open the door. However, I know many people who have spontaneously become spiritually aware in midlife — often but not always at a crisis point in their life.

I like to help others through this channel, where I am given guidance and information telepathically from my own guides, to help someone look at their own self and their future. Occasionally I do this using Angel cards. Angel cards are normally self-explanatory but when someone sees a card they have laid out in front of themselves, my guides help me explain why they should look at a particular area in their life so they can create their own future. This differs from Tarot cards which tend to reveal different options about your future.

As a Circle, we occasionally hold charity days. These are fun. Each of us does something different, giving taster sessions for a minimum fee. Some give healing, some use runes or animal cards. Some visitors come with an open mind, and others are more sceptical. I love doing readings for the latter; their faces when I suddenly hit on a sore spot or something I just could not have known are always a picture! If you believe in Angels, there are many packs to choose from which normally come with a guidance book. You can start giving readings to friends and family.

I also started to study Astrology, which has proved to be a fascinating way of learning more about oneself. Where you are born, as well as the time and date, are important; where the planets are at the actual time of birth makes a huge difference to the person you are. Astrology can show you your strengths and weaknesses. If you would like to have a chart done but don't know the time of your birth, write to the appropriate Local Authority as they all have records.

Everyone's chart is completely different. Each sign, and the planets' alignment, have a different significance. Where the sun, moon and major planets are in relation to the twelve houses shows you where your life can excel and dip, and your personality traits.

Fascinating information can be gained from having an astrology chart done. Cathy, our Circle leader, astounds me when she meets someone for the first time and can instantly tell them a great deal about themselves just from a few simple questions. People born under a particular birth sign will share certain traits. It is also worth remembering that life goes in seven-year cycles. Each cycle is a flow, a rhythm. You may feel it coming two years in advance, or two years later, as it builds, peaks and wanes. Think about the ages of seven (out of childhood), fourteen (teenage years), twenty-one (an important turning point) and twenty-eight; you will see that you suddenly started to look at life differently.

Major events can happen around certain cycles. For example, many people nearing their thirtieth birthday approach it with anxiety or even dread. They start looking for grey hairs and paying attention to the ads

Master Your Own Destiny

for wrinkle creams! They think their biological clock is ticking loudly, and may wonder whether they should choose their career over having children.

Astrologers call this period, between twenty-eight and thirty, 'Saturn Returns'. It is the first time that the planet Saturn completes the cycle through your birth chart and returns to the spot it occupied when you were born. Saturn can be a hard lesson but this is an important time of ending and new beginnings, usually a turning point. It can be a brilliant time for a new venture — but you may feel reluctant to let go of the security of what is familiar.

Lessons from the past need to be spring cleaned, otherwise you carry them with you and they come knocking on your door at the next Saturn Return — which is around the age of fifty-eight. By that time you are more settled in your ways, so it may be harder to change. Then again, there is the old saying that life begins at forty, so hopefully you will have learned to know the true you by then!

Forty-two is the polar opposite of the twenty-eight year stage. Back then, you viewed the world saying, *What can you give me?* At forty-two, you say, *What can I give the world?* It's a time of questioning.

It is a scientific fact that your physical body completely rebuilds itself over a seven-year cycle. Every bone cell, brain cell, skin and organs is replaced over this cycle.

You can also look at friends and family, as they are a reflection of yourself. You have drawn them into our lives for various reasons. They will mirror some of your qualities, and also the negative part of you. It can be hard to comprehend but often, when you criticise your friends or family members because of something annoying they have done or said, this is a reflection of something within yourself rather than about them. If they have a trait that doesn't bother you, then you have probably already worked through or outgrown that concept. This is what creates patience; its means you have mastered something which others are still working through.

Look at your own values and what is important in your life. What are your truths and are they reflected in the people who surround you?

Sometimes you do want to change — but it can feel uncomfortable. Change can be a scary place. You must be clear about the goals you set yourself. To be able to move forward you have to let go of the things that are not working in your life. You seem to hang on to those because they feel safe. But if they don't resonate with the person you are now, you have to let them go. When you focus on what you *want*, it makes this easier.

Be ambitious in your outlook. Nothing will change if you continue with your old patterns. Think about the habits you have now and how they affect every aspect of your life. You rarely think about them; you just do them.

- Your weight and health are determined by your eating and drinking habits.
- Your relationships with people are determined by your social habits.
- Your success at work or college is determined by your work habits.
- You even have buying habits; take a look around your house and at your clothes.
- The dictionary says that habit means 'an acquired behaviour pattern regularly followed until it has become almost involuntary'.
- Ask yourself: what do you do every week, day, or night that has become a habit? Does it bore you or excite you?
- How many hours do you sit in front of the television, socialise, or do something fun?

A good way to change a habit into something positive is to begin repeating an action, attitude or thought process every day for 21 days, or for up to 90 days depending on the habit. After a period of time they become permanent habits. Notice your responses to things and set yourself goals.

Examples of bad habits that the media always pick on are drinking and smoking. Start by cutting down, keep a diary and write your emotions about whether it was a good or bad day and why. See your new habits emerging so you can watch your progress. Even achieving one good new thing every day is wonderful progress. I know this from personal experience: whilst I am writing this book I am trying to give up smoking!

The importance of laughter

Fun and laughter are often overlooked when you get bogged down in daily life. Sometimes you are so stressed by what is going on 'outside' in your life that you forget the importance of what is going on 'inside'. Laughter is one of the most healing tools you have, literally at your fingertips.

Laughing has an energy that helps to dispel the stress, the worries and the fears in life. When you are in the moment and feeling overwhelmed, tired, or things are falling around you — take a break and do something that brings a little joy into your life. It won't take away your feelings but to break a pattern can help dispel the chaotic energy that has been created. One of the most important things is to learn to laugh *at yourself*. We all make mistakes and we are all human; to find humour in something silly can bring tears to your eyes which will then give you joy.

Life does *not* have to be serious. Your thoughts may make it seem so but life is to be enjoyed, not endured.

Let's recap...

STEP 1 — Meditate every day and keep a diary.

STEP 2 — Let go of fears, core conditioning and resistance.

STEP 3 — Practise visualisation and follow your instincts, hunches and sudden ideas.

STEP 4 — Believe in yourself. You are powerful beyond measure.

Praise and confidence are vital.

You are an individual soul who should have a wonderful belief in yourself. You are special; we all are. You are a spiritual being having a human experience — not the other way around. This is all part of your spiritual growth and evolving as the person you were meant to be, by learning some of the lessons you came here to experience. (There is more about this in Chapter Eight.)

You have the key to open your own door

Chapter Five

Appreciating life

A man is free at the moment he wishes to be.
— *Voltaire*

I have written a good deal about learning life's lessons. Sometimes I wonder whether you can ever know them all, or the reason why, until you go back to where you came from before you were born and agreed to come to the School of the Universe. Some lessons are simple for you; others have a major impact.

In the last few decades new ideas have come to the fore, suggesting that we are each creating our own dis-ease by our thoughts and even our habits. I agree *and* disagree with this.

When I was in my thirties I suddenly got a Malignant Melanoma, the most dangerous form of skin cancer. My doctor believes this stemmed from my years of travelling and lying in the sun all day, as I am fair haired and have a lot of moles. I'd noticed that a mole on my left arm had turned 'funny' and I was sent to a specialist who immediately did a biopsy and then told me it was cancerous and I needed a big operation.

I can't begin to describe the feeling you have when someone tells you that it is cancer. That sort of thing happens to other people, not to you. It's so scary, because I think it is the fear of the unknown which is the most daunting. I could not bear to consider the thoughts that came to me at the time: *will I die? will I survive? will it hurt? how big will the scar be? has it spread elsewhere, to give me secondary cancer, as it can travel especially to the lymph nodes? how will my family manage without me, such young children to lose their Mummy?*

Although my initial cancer was diagnosed more than 23 years ago, I can still remember this feeling because my skin cancer came back again very recently. What on earth do you do, at a time like that?

Master Your Own Destiny

Well, you *can* sit and cry all day from the shock; to respond in this way is perfectly understandable. Or you can steel your mind to overcome these thoughts — and that is the route I chose. Hard to do, I agree, but I couldn't let myself wallow in self-pity. This may seem a heartless thing for me to say — and indeed, I could write another book on my feelings and thoughts at that time, although I don't feel it's appropriate to go into details here — but it's the message that is important. We all deal with this situation differently … but you do have a choice. My heart goes out to anyone reading this, who is at that stage right now.

Following that first big operation I've had many other moles dealt with because they had 'turned' and had to be removed before they could become cancerous. Nearly every year, one or two would have to be dealt with. But I did have nine years in between, when everything was clear — or so I thought.

I was visiting my specialist about a particular mole on my left leg. As soon as I walked into the room he spotted something on my face and said: 'That will have to come off.' I'd thought it was just a bubble that had appeared from nowhere… it turned out to be Basal Cell Carcinoma. Then he discovered a Squamous Cell Carcinoma on the top of my leg, which shocked me. I had not exposed this part of my body to the sun for decades, so how could I have got this? (These are both different from a Malignant Melanoma but are still cancerous.)

When I got 'the big one' I was at the happiest time of my life; how I created this I am not sure. Plus, and this is a very big plus, my mother had a form a skin cancer and had to have a Rodent Ulcer removed from her leg. Unfortunately, when hers was dug out it left a big hole which was covered with a skin graft — but thankfully, cancer surgery has moved on and my own scar is not so traumatic.

But because two generations were affected, we were asked to take part in a clinical trial. This revealed that in our family we have a particular type of mole that is susceptible to becoming cancerous. My two children were both found to have a mole, in exactly the same place on their scalps, which is of the same type. So the gene runs in my family! Mine turned into cancer but hopefully for my children it won't.

This brought me back to my question: *How did I create this?* Could it be that we may have a gene that runs in families and our thoughts activate it? Thankfully none of my sisters has cancer, so what did *I* think to activate the cancer in me?

I have two theories. The first is that when I was travelling, sunning myself and splashing olive oil all over my skin, perhaps a fear did creep in. Skin cancer was unheard of when I was a child but was beginning to be recognised a few years later.

The second is that, when I was aged twelve to fifteen, I hated my moles and wished I had never had them. My Dad did say he would pay for them to be removed. However, that would have cost a fortune so I said no and learned to live with them. I never loved them but I did accept them — but deep down, did I really?

Now that I don't have many moles left to remove, I suspect the second theory may be true!

One of my Circle friends suggested a third possibility. She said that something deep inside of me was eating away at my flesh — what a horrible thought. I am one of the most placid people you will ever meet, and thoughts like that never enter my head. Moles are not of the flesh, they have roots — so I know *that* theory is wrong.

During the last ten years I've had another couple of cancer scares, including a lump in my breast and another in my womb. Thankfully, when investigated, they were both benign; I'm not sure I could have handled that on top of all the rest.

But this brings up another theory I have: *Do we know that we are going to suffer a serious illness before we come into this life?* Because to some people, it can be a blessing.

This may sound strange but often a serious illness helps you grow and will change your life. I know from my own experience that it helped me appreciate everything and everybody in my life as it puts life in perspective.

Some of those who find themselves given a short lifespan after a terminal diagnosis say that it gives them peace, after they have come to terms with it. They go on to live out their lives to the full, doing things they would never normally have done or even believed they could. Families may create a closer bond, making contact with each other for the first time in years.

Many paraplegic athletes do amazing things. Some are born disabled, others have had to adjust to a new life and find a determination they never knew they had. Sadly, there are also those who can never adjust.

These are only *my* thoughts and I know it is a delicate subject. I have been through cancer, and I still have it — but my mind cannot accept that it will ever get the better of me. I just won't let it! Do not imagine I have forgotten what it feels like; I haven't. But this is a difficult message and it can apply to anybody.

The thoughts I had as an early teenager, when I loathed my moles and wanted them removed, materialised many years later into the removal of them because of cancer. So my wishes and thoughts became true — but never as I expected. I now call it *the* cancer, not *my* cancer. A friend pointed this out to me recently: what you say in your speech is just as important as what you think because it is still in your mindset.

Cancer is one of many serious illnesses, and I hope I can give hope to many people who are living with any of those. You can get through a fatal disease — but how the mind processes the emotions is extremely important. I was in my mid-thirties when first diagnosed; I wasn't at all spiritual but I always had a deep inner knowing that I would be all right because I set my mind to say that to myself.

(Whilst writing this, my Angel has just touched me on my leg. That is beautiful, because she has remembered that that is exactly where the moles I most hated were — and I had forgotten that. I lived in black trousers because I didn't think I was beautiful.)

Louise Hay has written extensively on this subject, including *You Can Heal Your Life*. Her books are insightful and she has even turned this particular book into a film.

Something To Think About

- How have you dealt with something serious? (It need not be an illness.)
- How do you feel about this subject? Has it made you think?
- Do you dismiss the idea that we create our own illnesses?
- Do you appreciate your own life? How do you feel about it?

I believe this concept is true — but it leads me to question why I went through a couple of other things. One day I fell over in the garden and knocked my two front teeth out; what is *that* telling me? A lady with no front teeth is not a pretty sight!

I received third degree burns on my neck and chest when a bottle of 98 per cent sulphuric acid fell over and splashed me, leaving a horrible scar. People ask me if I've have ever had open heart surgery, because the scar runs down in a line. I did have plastic surgery to correct it but that went wrong and I had to hide indoors for six weeks until it healed. So I wonder ... are accidents different?

This brings up yet another question. Some people, meeting me for the first time, instantly notice my scar and react in one of two ways: either they ask me about it, or they look at it and then turn away for a few seconds after which they say nothing. Yet friends I have known for years have never even noticed it! They see beyond my scar to the beauty within.

How do *you* react when you see someone with a disability? My scar is very minor compared to some disfigurations that people live with. Do you see beyond that?

Many people, including Louise Hay, say that where a particular illness is located on your body tells you what it is connected to. For example, if you are having problems with your eyes, is there something you are not seeing? Do you get car sickness from a fear of being trapped? I can see the logic in this idea but I will leave this debate open for the time being, while I ponder more about what all my ailments were telling me!

One thing I do know is that, by acknowledging what is probably the root cause and going deep within to find that out, I have removed it. This is why I know my cancer will always be under control, and I know it won't come back.

In 2004 I watched a television documentary called *The Boy Whose Skin Fell Off*. The boy's name was Jonny Kennedy, and aged 36 he knew he was going to die. He had a terrible genetic condition called Dystrophic Epidermolysis Bullusa (EB) which meant that his skin literally fell off at the slightest touch, leaving his body covered in agonising sores and leading to his final fight with skin cancer.

This film touched millions of people. He made it to raise funds for the charities DebRA and EB but his message was his philosophy that death is part of life. He knew that he had come to what he called 'Earth is a classroom'; that he had been born, for whatever reason, to understand and feel suffering. He did not know why and it didn't matter — but his spiritual beliefs helped him come to terms with EB. His body was broken but his spirit was not. He even went to 10 Downing Street as he was dying to raise awareness.

Jonny's message is powerful. He and his family knew that he would be free from pain once his soul was released. I am sure he smiled, wherever he was, when he saw the reaction his film caused.

Dealing with challenges

How do you deal with some of the challenges that life throws at you? You often create your own challenges and we all deal with them in a different way. Some want too much, some think everyone around them has to be perfect. We all need to chill out.

Many people worry too much and are stressed beyond their boundaries. Life can be challenging but I hope that some of the previous chapters may have helped you see that you can be our own worst enemy! The most important chapter so far is Chapter Three, where you learned that the power of your mind can override some of your challenges.

I have found that the Universe will throw you a challenge or nudge you in a certain direction if you aren't listening to what 'they' are trying to tell you. Perhaps you'll continue on your way, struggling and getting frustrated and stressed, and then suddenly — *boom!* — something drastic happens.

Friends and colleagues of mine have had a sudden jolt, perhaps fallen over and broken a leg: or they might have a heart attack that stops them in their tracks and makes them take stock of their life. It's as if the Universe is saying, *You aren't listening or slowing down so we'll help you do that.* You then have to pay attention because you can't do anything else!

This is a time to reflect and take stock. You might need to ask others for help, or do the reverse and *let* someone help you. You do not have to struggle on your own. Your friends here on Earth and above in the Universe are all waiting to help — but you do have to ask. That is very difficult for some people: it feels like letting go of control. But often that is exactly why you are struggling.

If something like this has happened to you, it's important to let events unfold to bring certain things to your attention. What could this be teaching you? What might you need to let go? This sort of event can be a painful or a healing process. You *could* just carry on as before — but why do that?

There is another aspect I would like to put to you. We constantly shout at our children when they misbehave. (There is more on this towards the end of the book.) We fall out with friends and neighbours if they do or say something we dislike. Why? Everyone has different views and ideas, which are unique to them. We may not agree with someone but why never speak to that person again? When anger and resentment build up inside us, it is we who then suffer, not them!

Anger, jealousy, resentment, envy and all the negative emotions to which you expose yourself create a world for you that can be unrealistic. You build your own obstacles. You might not be living your own life, because you are comparing yourself to others.

Many people also hold on to resentment for far too long. It begins to eat away at them. From the day they have their *Aha!* moment and let go, life is never the same again. It can be a liberating release. Dwelling on the dark side of life can lead to depression. So, you need to ask ourselves what good it does.

Often, people don't realise they are in an emotional cage; a very lonely place. They may have gone into that cage for self protection and do not know that they have closed their own door. Try coming out of it but gradually. To open your heart and show your emotions can be very difficult but do you want to stay in your confined closed closet?

This is different to understanding that the positive and negative need each other in order to exist. Without the dark side your beauty would not exist. How can you compare if you don't have both?

One of the best ways I have found to deal with challenges is to keep my faith by 'going with my flow'. I let some of the little things fly over my head. Many people can't do that, I know, but I want to turn this around and put it in a different perspective. Here are a few questions:

- Who is the most important person in your life?
- What gives you the most pleasure?
- What is missing in your life?
- What or who drains your energy?
- What do you like, and dislike, about your life you could change?
- What has been your biggest success to date?
- What have you contributed to the world that will make a difference?

By answering these questions I hope you can begin to see that life is far more beautiful if you appreciate it rather than moan about everything. Yes, bills have to be paid, health problems crop up and life does sometimes become painful — but so often you forget the wonderful things you do have. Friends and family need to be cherished. Our gardens, the parks, the mountains and nature are all around us to enjoy. How often do you do this?

We tend to concentrate on problems rather than the highs in life. So, here are a few suggestions:

- Let go of control — you don't have to control or do everything yourself.
- People will not hate you if you say *no* occasionally.
- Delegate where you can — even at home with the children.
- Others will not think you are pathetic if you ask for help occasionally.
- Prioritise your diary — block out some time for you.
- Give yourself time to rest and relax by having some 'me' time — and don't feel guilty.
- Practise patience — life is not a race.
- Communicate with others more — work colleagues, family and friends.

- Share meals around the table and chat and laugh!
- Forget what you don't have — appreciate what you do have.
- Self control: to get angry is human — but to express it properly is effective.
- What worry changed anything? Go with your flow more and see the benefits.
- Never be too busy to listen to others — especially your children and family.
- Focus on what motivates you rather than look at the negatives.
- Stop repeating negative patterns and you will move on faster than you think.
- Deal with a challenge instead of hiding from it, as it may not go away.

Oh no

I knew another challenge was on the horizon after a spiritual Circle one night (see Chapter Eight) when an Angel, 'Sister of Mercy', came to see me.

A 'Sister of Mercy' will often come when an emotional pain is looming and she comes to comfort you. Anthony, one of the Circle members, had done a Tarot reading for me but he felt sick with what he saw in the cards. He didn't know what was going to happen and neither did I.

The next day my five-year-old granddaughter came to see me in floods of tears, saying she wanted to live with me. She had packed her own little bags because my daughter and she were at constant loggerheads and she was unhappy at home. It broke my heart but I had to say no. My daughter then took me to court to stop me seeing her. The pain of this separation nearly drove me insane. My granddaughter suffered horrendously too. We were separated for three long years and it took another two years for everything to be resolved, and they both came back into my life.

I will not go into details here (it is all in my other book) because they are now completely back in my life which is wonderful, joyous and a true blessing. It would be dragging up the past and I don't want to do that, for me or for them.

But I do need to mention it here because one of the best ways for me to deal with that horrendous challenge was to keep my faith and to learn forgiveness. Learning forgiveness is one of the hardest and yet most important lessons we can learn. Having my 'unseen' friends around was beyond doubt what kept me going; they gave me courage and a strength I never knew I had. But I also learned to look within, because I was so afraid of what might happen if I never saw my granddaughter again.

Then I learned to stop resisting that pain, because in some ways I was fighting my own fears. The negativity that was going on in my head was awful — but when I recognised that my fear was only making it worse for me, I began to know somehow that it would all work out. And it did. I also learned another valuable lesson which was to forgive my daughter and myself for the creation of this experience. I can't explain it any other way.

In fact, after I learned to work through my grief, which is what this painful experience felt like, I trusted and detached myself from the end result. I had started gradually to get back on track when suddenly both my daughter and granddaughter came back into my life, years earlier than I had imagined possible. The timing was amazing because it coincided with my first book coming out — so I knew that everything would be fine.

Sometimes you need to detach yourself, and let both parties work through their thoughts and emotions separately. When you stop *reacting* to a situation it helps calm everything down. This can be extremely hard to do. You need to give each other space. Everyone goes through things differently; outside events often play a part, and of course you may not know about them. You don't know how people are truly feeling and you never can   however much you like to think you do.

Another reason why I went through all this was to be able to understand how to cope so I can help others — that is why I wrote my first book. So many people are separated from loved ones, for all sorts of reasons, and statistics say that something like this will happen to around 60 per cent of the population — in other words, to millions of people. I became a volunteer for the Grandparents Association on their helplines, and what I heard on the end of the phone astounded me. The GA was my lifeline at the very beginning, and this was my way of saying thank you for the help they gave me.

I also know that this book has inspired others because of the feedback I have had, when people write to me or ring me up in tears, saying how they can resonate with it.

Something wonderful happened a few months after the release of my first book. A lady at an exhibition tapped me on the shoulder and said: 'You won't remember me but I can never thank you enough because you changed my life. I came to a talk you did and I read your book and it gave me the strength and courage to do something I should have done years ago. Thank you from the bottom of my heart as I now feel so alive.'

Wow. I burst into tears and so did she! Her friend told me that she'd read it too, and it had helped her with problems she had been having in her family — so I got a cuddle from her, too. That sort of experience makes everything worthwhile.

So, however painful it was for me, there was a *reason*. There's nearly always a reason that you can't see at the time. But keep your faith, learn from it and embrace with joy the new that comes into your life.

Spontaneous gestures

I am not being flippant about dealing with life's challenges; they can take over your life if you let them — and they often do until you learn to work through the experience. However, I would like to point out that another way to deal with life is to have something which a lot of people seem to have forgotten — fun. Take some time out of your everyday life to do something different, which will take your mind off your problems and give you a much-needed lift. Life doesn't have to be so serious!

One of the things I love to do is give spontaneous gestures to friends and family when they least expect it. It brings smiles all around and gives me great joy.

When I visit my grandchildren and I bring sweets, instead of just giving them I hide them in the garden to find. Why keep an Easter egg hunt (which I also do) just for Easter? The children love it and the sweets only cost a few pence.

Another idea I had one day brought even more response. I came across Graham's car at his place of work. So I wrote a note on a scrap of paper — with rather a sexy message! It was raining so I found a plastic bag and placed the note inside before tucking it under his windscreen wipers, just as traffic wardens do.

Of course, his first thought when he saw this was dread of a parking ticket — but then he got a wonderful surprise which certainly put a smile on his face. He says he found this gesture exciting and that it had aroused such emotions that he landed up on my doorstep, after travelling along the motorway at high speed, and simply carried me upstairs. I will leave the rest to your imagination!

I once told this story as part of a presentation to a group of ladies, some of whom were quite elderly. Along with the laughter was a lady of about 70 sitting on my right, who was so engrossed in the story that her instant reaction was to shout out: 'But I don't have any stairs.' This brought the house down. After some giggly banter, we all decided that her sofa and downstairs bedroom would serve just as well … but I have no idea whether she put the idea into action when she got home!

Putting fun back into your life can be deeply beneficial. You don't always need to concentrate of the challenges or on what you haven't got. There is far more, deep inside you, that you should give yourself credit for.

Putting excitement into life doesn't need to be expensive — just imaginative.

Stop those relationship disasters

Something I learned a long time ago is to have honest conversations.

This can be hard because you often don't want to hurt a person — but sometimes not knowing is harder to bear than being honest and knowing the truth. Your imagination may run riot but there are always two sides to a situation; knowing the other half can dispel your fears.

Even saying how you feel, perhaps that you love the other person, can move mountains. So often you can't say those three little words.

But you do need to be careful with the words you choose to express your thoughts. Words can hurt deeply but there are times when it is better to be honest. Shouting your anger will only backfire on you — so be gentle but firm.

Importantly, you must *not* feel that meeting the perfect partner will be the answer to your happiness. You have to love yourself first and then, if a partner is what you want, when you do meet him or her, you will be in the strongest position to work at it.

You have to accept your partners just as they are, and accept that you cannot change them. They are the person you originally fell in love with, before you knew their faults, and you need to go on accepting and loving them just as they are.

Some couples may find that, with time, their relationship gets to become a habit; they merely exist with one another. It's as though the spark that they had first felt has died. For most couples those initial feelings *don't* last forever; what they achieve instead is a feeling of contentment. People do change — but if you work at it, and if you want it enough, you have the power within to change and move the relationship on and put some excitement back in.

Creating excitement does not have to be expensive but a little surprise can go a long way. A spontaneous gesture such as the one I mentioned earlier can be wonderful. It brings excitement and interest back into a relationship.

I can hear some of you saying, *It is such hard work…* or, *I have not got the time…* or even, *I can't be bothered…* A little effort goes a long, long way and creating excitement really does need only a small amount of imagination. Focus on the *benefit* of this 'effort', as it is sure to improve your relationship.

Too many couples get into such a rut that it is hard for them to pull out of it. It's almost as though they do not even want to. This is such a shame because at the beginning of the relationship, perhaps many years ago, they will have been head-over-heels in love.

Relationship exercise

Do you ever feel as though you and your partner are moving in different directions or failing to understand each other and consider each others needs? This exercise shows you how you can re-connect with that special person in your life.

Sit down together and just talk about your feelings. Then, over the next week, separately make a list of five to ten things that you each want out of the relationship. Make another list, of all the things that you love about the other person, and then write down some of the things that have changed over the years. Take your time. When you both have your lists ready, arrange some quality time when there will be just the two of you, and spend the evening discussing each and every item on each list.

I hope this activity enables you both to discuss openly the key elements of your relationship. I also hope that it encourages mutual respect.

You will probably find that other issues come out, which are not on your lists; it may be painful to discuss these. However, if someone is unhappy, surely it is better to talk about problems and feelings, rather than just hiding them? This is when so often things start to go wrong in long term relationships. This can help rebuild the relationship and is a very worthwhile exercise.

Some people in a partnership or marriage will say: 'I love them, but...' They think they can change that person into who they want them to be. I'm sorry — but no. No-one can change a person, only they can do this for themselves, and even then only if they want to. We just need to accept our partners as they are.

Maybe it is something insignificant that you want to change; perhaps one of you wants to take a lot of time out of the week to pursue a personal interest. For example, your partner might be passionate about sport, and want to watch *all* sports on the television, go to support their club or team and play sports themselves. You might resent this — but by viewing this 'annoying' situation differently and taking a step back, you could come to see this as a brilliant opportunity for you to spend time away from each other, which you can use as quality time for *you*. After all, your partner is enjoying their quality time, so why shouldn't you? Accept that it happens and join in, or simply plan to do something else which you enjoy and may not normally have the time to pursue. Isn't this more fulfilling than resenting your partner and their interests?

Everyone needs a little time to themselves, even if it is just for a few hours each week. You should never feel guilty about quality time for yourself. It gives you space, an escape from a lot of the pressures, and it is surprising how it makes you feel. You will find yourself feeling more relaxed and refreshed when you have more time for your thoughts and actions. You will be able to achieve more, and be in a better position to enjoy the time you do spend with your partner.

So many people think that they don't have time to do this sort of thing — but what are you saying when you don't make time for yourself? That you don't matter? Or that your needs are not important? I don't think so!

Let's recap...

STEP 1 — Meditate every day and keep a diary.

STEP 2 — Let go of fears, core conditioning and resistance.

STEP 3 — Practise visualisation and follow your instincts, hunches and sudden ideas.

STEP 4 — Believe in yourself.

STEP 5 — Rise to a challenge. Overcome obstacles and have some fun.

Overcoming challenges, whether it is an illness or another major obstacle, can be a huge step forward.

Many spiritual gurus have been teaching for years that to learn forgiveness is probably one of the most important lessons you can learn for your spiritual growth — and I have found this to be very true. It can be hard but you sometimes need to forgive *yourself*, too.

You also need to work at relationships to bring them back to the joy they were. This is important. Everyone changes as they get older but the core person is still inside.

Appreciating Your Life

Chapter Six

The Grand Design

My life is my message.
— Mahatma Ghandi

Life never ceases to amaze me.

Another incident that made me see that my life had been mapped out for me happened at the start of writing my first book. When I sat down at my computer to write the words of my letter, little did I know that my whole life was about to change!

I had decided to down-size when the children left home, and eighteen months later I fell in love with a beautiful fifteenth-century cottage with vaulted ceilings. The moment I walked in I felt at home.

But the house I was living in hadn't sold, so I arranged a buy-to-let mortgage and planned to rent it out. But no-one wanted to live there for six months — so, was I mad to go ahead? I could not bear to give up my new cottage so I just went with my flow. It felt right at the time but I am sure many of my friends thought I had lost the plot! Two houses are expensive to run.

Then two doctors turned up who wanted to rent it; so all was well. This was around the time I became unemployed when I left BUPA but then they asked me to go back as a consultant. That contract brought in some decent money so I could keep things afloat until I found another job — or so I thought.

Nine months later, at exactly the same time as the idea of turning my letter into a book hit me, out of the blue I received an offer of the full asking price for my old house. It just so happened that this windfall would be enough to keep me going until my book was published. It enabled me to take time out to continue with my writing and launch my new business — which I didn't realise at the time I was about to do but 'they' up above knew what was going to happen. The timing of all this was remarkable.

My inner guidance system had been gently nudging me in the right direction. When I look back now it seems incredible that when you follow your heart, listen to the sudden ideas which pop into your head, or take a gamble, it all works out as it should. I am now, thanks to the Universe, living my dream; and all because the Universe, my spiritual helpers, guided me to where I was meant to be. 'They' could see the bigger picture as I could not.

This was a powerful lesson. Suddenly synchronicity was at work, and I watched my life unfold. So many new doors opened where I was expecting none. My publishers made me their first Featured Author on their UK website, with a write-up about my success. A lady from Ottakars where I did my first signing recommended me to give some talks at a huge book festival my local council was running called 'Word on the Street' — and I was among some top writers there. The phone kept ringing from different BBC local radio stations asking to interview me. This was exciting.

During the first workshop I did at this time, I realised that it was exactly fifteen years to the day that my husband had left; if that had not happened I wouldn't have been doing all of this.

Life was about to get even better. People who were beginning to open up spiritually started to ask me for coaching and I loved helping them. To watch people start to glow, and to understand what is happening to them, is bliss. But could I coach *myself* into giving a twist to my talking career? Now, that was different!

It is often easier to give guidance to someone else than to oneself. I tossed and turned at night, waking up in cold sweats. All my talks, except those written for Mind Body Soul events, were purely about personal development. I wasn't including anything spiritual because of my fear of being considered deranged. Popular speakers such as Dr Wayne W Dyer and Louise Hay were doing sell-out gigs but they were already well known and had been doing this for years.

How could I approach event organisers saying I wanted to give a talk but that it had a spiritual aspect, and by the way I was fairly new at all this?

I made a very bold decision which I can only describe as being like 'coming out' as a gay person. Announcing my spiritual side to the world — or, should I say, to my work colleagues — was a huge step.

Afterwards, I wondered why I had left it so long! People approached me at meetings after my brief thirty-second introduction, and said they could resonate with me. They would say it incredibly quietly. It dawned on me that because *I* said it quietly, they did too. As soon as I became bolder and more candid about it, work started flooding in.

Everyone kept telling me that successful people have a niche in which they are experts. Where was I going to find *my* market? Suddenly, the Universe started sending people to me instead of me looking for them! Of course, I still had to market myself but it was getting easier. It wasn't that I was concentrating on becoming rich and famous — because to me the important thing was to get my message out there, and to help people who could turn their own lives around.

Then it came to me: I knew far more than I realised and I could in fact become an expert. I was taking my spiritual experiences for granted — but that meant I had a unique message and a unique niche for my talks!

So often we take for granted something we are good at, and assume that 'everyone knows that'. No, they don't. *You* do because that is what you have become an expert in!

Nick Williams was an inspiration for me again, and now everything he had always told me suddenly made sense. So, I joined his Entrepreneurs Club where he runs courses about how to take your expertise out into the big wide world. He and his business partner Niki Hignett are passionate about this, and now so am I.

We all have knowledge in our heads that we need to share with others, in business and in our everyday lives.

Point To Ponder

- What do you know, that you could share with others?
- What skills do you possess which you could use?
- Could your turn your knowledge into a business?
- Could you teach?
- Could you write articles to help others or start a blog?
- Could you volunteer at a local association of interest?

- Can you see potential in your friends and family and encourage them to explore how they could share *their* knowledge?
- To gain even more knowledge could you attend a course, read a book or study at home or college?

There are courses in every subject you can think of nowadays. Day, weekend or even residential courses are available. The Internet or your local libraries are good places to start. When you put this thought out to the Universe you may find that suddenly a friend will recommend a course or a book! Don't forget that often your friends share the same interests, so that isn't such a silly idea.

Sharing knowledge with a group of people or friends, or starting a new business, is a skill. You have to listen to both sides, and not insist that your way is best. Other people have learned things too and may have a completely different point of view; you have to stay open to learning more in the process. Be gentle in how you share your knowledge.

Expanding my business

Having a foot in both worlds and 'coming out' as a spiritual guru meant some things had to change. My website aspirations4u was no longer relevant, for two reasons. Firstly, everyone who Googled me did so under my name and not the company name. Secondly, Theresa was being called in a different direction in her own work life. It was time for a change.

So, I began to market myself under my own name, redesigned the website and changed all my marketing material. No small task! I found a company in London who redesigned my logo at a very reasonable cost. However, I found making all these decisions on my own rather stressful. I would bounce ideas off friends and colleagues but the final decision still rested with me. I can't tell you how many times I rewrote my website, the flyers and the main marketing material. It all took months.

I decided to capture the contact details of people who visited my website and attended my talks — so I started a newsletter. At my talks

I handed around a sheet for people to add their email addresses. I also added Google Analytics™ to my website; this is an excellent free tool which tells you who is looking at it, the referring sites, how long they spend on each page and the average visit time.

At this point I have to contradict some experts in this field: if people are interested in what they are reading they will take the time to study it. My average visitor spends between five and nine minutes reading between five and six pages. I can get lots of useful information from Google Analytics and I am sure there are other sites offering something similar.

The newsletter is a great way to capture names but it needs to offer something in return. A free 'tips sheet' or booklet, or a free e-course, are all valuable assets which will attract people to sign up. My mailing list has grown, and every name is a potential client. I can then inform them of my next workshop and give them information on various different subjects so that they begin to build up a feeling of trust with me.

There were so many other things to do. People kept telling me I should create an Internet presence through the various new business networking sites that were springing up, so I have started doing that by creating a blog. I also needed to put my profile on to connection websites — but all in good time. I'm still working on the last one as I write this book. There is so much to think about and keeping up with it all is quite daunting sometimes.

All experiences, in whatever job or vocation you are in, are about learning and growing within yourself — not just for a business to grow.

Life path stages

This life path that you are on is uniquely personal for you.

We each have different experiences from which we need to learn. Some of us are here just to learn how to deal with an emotion such as anger, or to be loved which during a past life we might not have mastered. Others have much bigger challenges which we will look at in more depth in Chapter Eight. But not everyone has a grand business or working life plan: to be a home-maker, unemployed or a worker for others is just as important in the blueprint of anyone's life.

To feel complete inside, in whatever capacity in life, is all part of walking your truth and living out your grand plan. You may not need to reach big goals because you might be there already. That 'inner-knowing' and being content are all you need. To have personal wealth is far more rewarding than financial wealth; to have both is a bonus.

Many people will never want to evolve spiritually and will never become interested. This probably applies to the majority of the population. However, many people *are* beginning to wake up and become interested; they suddenly want to read books, attend courses or visit exhibitions. This is called the Exploration Stage.

You may become aware of being at a crossroads, of feeling that there is more to life than just materialism, of feeling empty. You want to move on but don't yet know how. At this point you might begin to consider a new path, even retrain and start a new career. Your curiosity is beginning to take hold. You might never pass this stage — but if it has satisfied your need, that is fine.

For some people, a new path suddenly appears which excites them. Their quest for knowledge begins to consume them. They may have started to experience some 'odd' sensations, had visions in pictures, or just find themselves increasingly happy to follow their intuition. They begin to have an inner-knowing, which is their awakening.

A lot of people don't realise that we all have spiritual gifts whether we like it or not! Everyone is born with psychic ability but you have the choice as to whether to open it or leave it closed. My advice is that the best way to open it is through meditation. By all means learn all you can through talking to people or reading — but you don't have to hear or see Angels, guides or ghosts to become spiritual. This is a process I call your inner-knowing; you are living your truth and serenity begins to set in.

Not everyone will ever develop their 'gift', as it is called. However, we all have certain qualities which may explain a few things you have noticed in yourself, and help you to see it in others. This will help you understand how you communicate. There are various ways of looking at this — for example NLP calls each area something similar — but for this exercise I will stick to the spiritual angle.

Healers — inner feelings
You or they have an intuitive need to help others. You'll be bubbly and inspire and want to help people feel good about themselves. You realise that people are more than just a person.

Prophecy — inner knowing
You or they will have hunches, pick up feelings, see the bigger picture all at the same time. People like this make good managers.

Clairvoyant — inner vision
You or they will see life in pictures, will love words, and love to read and learn. People like this see the whole picture and are natural leaders. They see it in their mind and can create it.

Clairaudience — inner thoughts and ideas
You or they will listen and hear. People like this have thoughts and ideas and have all the facts: what, when, where and why. They have the ability to keep things simple.

Some people will have all these gifts rolled into one. Everyone has all of these gifts to an extent — but you need to work out which is more prominent in your own case. Once you decide which main gift you have, and what you see as other people's gifts, you can begin to understand how their minds work. This then helps you to understand how to get the best out of others and it becomes easier to deal with people.

Try and work this out on some of the people you know in your life. I think you will find it fascinating

The grand design of my own life is continuing on a daily basis. I am consciously aware of whenever another jigsaw piece pops into place, or synchronicity pops up again, and I love it. Let me share with you now the story of a girl I met while I was giving a small talk.

This girl, in her early twenties, had done a five-year vision board and was delighted to tell me that she had achieved everything on there except one. She had learned to speak French, ridden in a helicopter and achieved several outstanding things she had wanted to do; and all in less than five years.

The one thing she *hadn't* achieved was to have a child. She'd had no idea, until the day she decided to have an honest conversation with him, that her partner of seven years didn't want children and that it was certainly not part of *his* life's plan. So what should she do; stay or leave him? She had done everything else on that vision board and was ready to do another five-year one — but this child might not be on there if she stayed with this partner.

I met her once she had done this new board, and her boyfriend was not on there. She had decided that it was better to know now, while she was still young enough to have children, to find a new man who wanted the same things in life and had the same values. It was a huge decision but she said that it inspired her to achieve even more in life. Even if she never has children, she has decided that that is part of her journey — and at least she would know and not regret it.

She will go far in life because of her foresight to have honest conversations and keep focused. She loved her boyfriend so it wasn't an easy decision — but she found it a liberating move because new doors suddenly opened for her. She had recently moved into her own house and was doing amazing things in the garden; she was all by herself but the satisfaction overrode every other feeling she had.

A *vision board* is a highly effective way of living your dream. As with *affirmations*, which we talked about earlier, and *goal setting* which we will cover in the next chapter, these are all part of the same context: getting the most from your life, including fun.

I am going to say something profound here: happiness is a choice, and success is a choice. Success and happiness come from just *being*. Finding peace is not a conclusion. These are all things which are simply a state of arrival. It is like creating a wonderful garden: there is no end to the nurturing and love needed but you do it with a richness you can find nowhere else other than within. That is why it's so important to have fun.

So, let's see what you can put on your own vision board, to inspire and make you more playful! One thing I do know is that your guardian Angel will be by your side when you do this, because that is what they are all about: fun.

Vision board or wish list

Most people do this by cutting out pictures from a magazine and sticking them on a cork board. Put in images representing all the things you want to achieve or do within the next five years. Don't make it all financial: include relationships, feelings and some fun. A big house, a new car, flying a plane, learning a new language, seeing a particular show, a special place you want to visit are all examples. You can also put in there how much you want to earn; break it down into a monthly figure if you want to but keep it realistic. You won't be a millionaire in five years if you earn £20,000 a year now but aim high. (You can include that on the next one five years from now!)

I also like to type or write little things which can't be explained in a picture, and pin them on there. Or you may like just to make a wish list. Put it somewhere you can see it every day. A friend of mine put hers in the bathroom and then had to take it out because all her visitors kept asking questions about it!

When you have achieved something, don't take it off the board. Tick it or mark it in some way, so that you can look back and be inspired when you do another one in five years time. These really work but you have to keep focused. Add to it if you want as your desires change, or do another board.

Something else you can do is create an imaginary bank account. Add to it daily or weekly but put in there something like £1,000 a day or per week and watch it mount up. Put beside the amount how you earn it and what you spent it on. Weekends away, a special treat, heating bills, going out are all good expenditures! It's fun but it works if you are sincere, and again you keep your focus.

As I write this chapter, I have to say that my own jigsaw puzzle is not yet fully complete because there are still two pieces missing. One is a distinguished grey-haired man that I keep 'seeing' in my meditations and visions, who I know is close now. 'They' have shown him to me many times over the last few years, including only a few weeks ago a picture of him walking up my garden path, in the sunshine with his shirt sleeves rolled up! This is getting frustrating, because many of my clairvoyant friends have 'seen' him too but for some reason he and I have not yet met.

I do know that he is part of the grand plan that I created before I arrived here on Earth. I know that the Universe will bring him to me when the time is right. I have waited a long time but I would rather wait for the right person, with whom I can share my life as an equal partnership, rather than make do with someone second-best, just for the sake of it!

Again, this comes down to trust. I suppose that, deep within, I may have to work through different scenarios to bring him into my life — but I can feel his presence and my instinct tells me it won't be long. I also believe that sometimes events and things can take years to materialise, rather than weeks or months as some experts will tell you. If this man had come into my life last year, for example, in hindsight it would not have been right because I would not be writing this book! When you look back over parts of your life you often discover the reason.

The other jigsaw piece that is missing is where my work is going to take me. This is always evolving and expanding, which is exciting. I have made a conscious decision not to play small in the world anymore. So many people, like myself, are frightened of success or of exposing themselves, of failing and making mistakes. I have learned that playing small serves no purpose: I have to trust that synchronicity will come into play again and it will! All the experiences I have been through are not just for me; I have to share hope with others.

I know that the last two pieces will suddenly fall into place because my instinct tells me and my intuition is screaming at me that they will both happen — so I am going with my flow again. However much I would like to, I can't rush this.

Mind you, I hate that phrase, *When the time is right*. We all get impatient at times but that is a great lesson we have to learn. In the Universe there is no such thing as *time*. We will cover this, and why we come here to planet Earth later, in Chapter Eight — but before we move on I will say that a spiritual path is not just a faith or a belief. It is a way of life.

We should all enjoy this journey because there is a reason why you are living at this time. To embrace it with joy, fun, open mindedness, compassion, exploration, co-creation, happiness and continual learning is all part of the process. No-one (and I really mean *no-one*) should suffer in life for no apparent reason.

Hardship is difficult to understand and you may never know the reason why until you return to your true home — but hardship and misery are two completely different concepts. Misery is something you can often change, because it exists in your mind. You can move away from something that makes you unhappy. You have a choice. Hardship in some parts of the world is very hard for us to get our heads around; only the Universe knows the true meanings behind those who suffer. We do create some of it ourselves with our greed, because what we do in the West affects elsewhere by destroying other parts of the Universe.

The grand design of your life evolves every day without you realising it. You may remember me saying in Chapter Three that *What you think you create*; well, you are going on this journey whether you realise it or not. You may as well make it as good as it can be.

I would like to ask you a question: if at the end of your life I asked you whether it had been a success, would you answer yes?

What would you like someone to say about you after you've gone? Hopefully, that your life has been full of everything you ever wanted to do and that you felt fulfilled. Before you answer those questions, here is something I have created which I hope *I* can truly say:

1. I awakened to the meaning of my life and lived in joy.
2. I enjoyed a long lasting, creative, 50/50 loving relationship with a man.
3. I learned to share and value everything and every moment in my life, and the wonders of the world never ceased to amaze me.
4. I valued every single friend who came into my life, along with my family.
5. I loved every written word I wrote and loved all the people I helped.
6. I developed an understanding of the creator of all life.
7. I rest in my bliss but know that I will continue my work from beyond.

I don't think I will change this much over the next years of my life but may tweak and add to it as my life evolves. What would *you* write?

The reason to write or to think about death — however uncomfortable that may be for you — is that it is a certainty just as your birth was. Your soul is well prepared for it but are you? We will cover this more in Chapter Eight.

Freedom and free will

A housewife, a business man or woman, self-employed, unemployed, teenager or child and every other human variety living on the planet … they are no different from each other. We all travel through different stages and want different things but ultimately we are all the same. What you want from life, however, may be completely different.

Some people are ambitious; others have no ambition at all, which believe it or not is just fine. You have choices and freedom to do as you wish. Freedom of choice is probably one of the most precious assets we have here in the West, and it is so often forgotten or taken for granted. People in many parts of the world have no freedom to choose.

If you have never experienced the horror of war, the solitude of prison, the pain of torture, suffered near-starvation or been too petrified to go to your place of worship, then respect your freedom. To be able to read this book in the comfort of your own home is a gift many people would give an indescribable gratitude to be able to do. They cannot see or have no home.

That is why it is so important to live your life with joy. We all have freewill and can make choices. How many of you reading that last paragraph will just dismiss it saying, *Oh, that happens to others, not to me.* No — you are one of the lucky ones. When you learn to love the inner you and appreciate the freedom and freewill you have, that is when you begin to see your flower open and grow into full blossom.

You are never judged by your spiritual helpers so why do you so often judge others? The biggest blessing you can give yourself is love. To love yourself and to love others is the greatest gift in the grand design of your life. When you learn that love, in the true sense of the word, is the most important thing on Earth, you bring serenity into your life and to others surrounding you.

Let's recap...

STEP 1 — Meditate every day and keep a diary.

STEP 2 — Let go of fears, core conditioning and resistance.

STEP 3 — Practise visualisation and follow your instincts, hunches and sudden ideas.

STEP 4 — Believe in yourself.

STEP 5 — Rise to a challenge. Overcome obstacles and have some fun.

STEP 6 — Your life has a blueprint so let your life unfold as it should be.

Don't fight and struggle or live in the past. Move on to the future with open eyes.

Enjoy the freedom that life has given you. Live in joy with love that surrounds you, and you create. Love is the most previous gift on Earth.

Follow Your Own Path

Chapter Seven

Goal setting

Imagination is everything. It is the preview of life's coming attractions.
— *Albert Einstein*

When I need spurring on, I find that nothing beats *goal setting*. It gives me focus and makes me get off my backside instead of sitting with excuses. When Julie gave me the free stand at her exhibition, for the launch of my first book, I had deadlines to meet which put everything into perspective. Suddenly I was running around in a frenzy of activity.

With this book I have set myself goals which the publishers have agreed with, and I have lined up an artist and editor. The rest is up to me. Because I have a deadline, time and people to help who have busy schedules, I know that I can't afford to flounder any more.

Hard as it might be to believe, I have sat and distracted myself often over the last few months. I tell myself, *Oh, I'll do it when I get inspired* or, *I'll get round to it when I have done such-and-such.* Friends pop around for a coffee or a glass of wine and how can I say no? This was all very well for a while — but then suddenly I understood what it was that I wanted. Everything snapped into focus and once that happened there was no stopping me!

Then I remembered another goal I had set myself some time before, which was to get my book out there again after all the initial publicity had died down. I had done lots of radio interviews, been in the Press, and sold many copies. However, it turns out that when a book has been out for a few months people lose interest; you have to reinvent yourself and your book. The alternative is to leave it on the shelf, and just plug it here and there when the opportunity arises. I wanted interest in my book to be revived in style. What I did about it was not the usual thing at all.

It occurred to me that the part of the book that told of the big separation from my granddaughter now had a happy ending — because my family was back in my life. So I re-wrote the last chapter creating a new second edition. Every group or trade has a charity week or day; I knew from my volunteer work with the Grandparents Association that and grandparents are one of them. This provided me with a brilliant hook for a news release aimed at the grandparents market.

I had been introduced to Becky, someone who could help me with the publicity I wanted. She was a young girl starting out in her own business but like me she had vision. We discussed my idea and it became clear that this was an exciting project for both of us. We were not sure whether we could pull it all off — but Becky could certainly get me some radio interviews and Press coverage. The angle for the press release was that my situation now had a happy ending.

Many press releases about books don't have an up-to-date news connection; mine did. We were working towards a week in September — Grandparents Week — and it was May now, so there was plenty of time. Magazines usually work three or more months in advance, other media are more last-minute.

We discussed what to put in the press release, drafted and re-drafted it. Finally it was sent out at the beginning of July to those parts of the Press with deadlines way ahead of the charity week. We were saving the bigger ones such as television and radio for nearer the time. Becky made all the follow-up calls as the phone began to ring. I did some Radio interviews and a few articles appeared in magazines — but secretly I was aiming higher.

The next set of press releases was sent out, triggering the series of hair-raising, nail-biting moments that followed. Becky took a call from someone she knew at ITV: they were considering, but only *considering*, doing a piece on me. It's hard to describe the excitement we both felt. Becky had never succeeded in getting anyone on TV before. I had secretly aimed high for a reason.

Some time before, I had laughingly put out a request to the Universe for this to happen but I hadn't mentioned it to Becky. Then, suddenly, I had been shown by my spiritual helpers quite a few pictures in my mind of me on television. I could see 'pictures' of myself going to the studio — but occasionally the picture had an audience. I could see the people sitting there and their faces; I kept visualising it over and over again because I didn't want to lose this.

I had also been told (by my guides) that the show I would be on would be *Richard & Judy*, however they were taking a break from broadcasting so I wasn't sure about that detail. Friends had also been telling me *they* had 'seen' me on *Richard & Judy* so I wasn't sure what was going on — but again I just 'went with the flow'. We heard nothing more for ages. Becky learned that her friend had left the studio, so we just prayed and kept our fingers crossed. The prayers we sent out must have been heard because her friend did pass on our press release — but we did not know to whom at this point. A week later we got a call from ITV to say that *This Morning* were very interested in me coming to the studio and was I available…

I discussed the details with a researcher. Because of the nature of the interview my daughter, ex-husband and son all had to give their permission in case they were mentioned. They all gave their blessing and the arrangements were made.

I knew what I was going to wear, to match my pink and black book covers. However, I needed a new necklace to finish off the outfit, so a friend Janice and I went on a shopping spree and purchased one. Not being sure how I would react to being on television, I also bought myself some of Dr Bach's Flower Rescue Remedy, which is a natural product and an effective way to calm oneself down.

Another phone call came through: would I drop in for a chat with Sharon Osborne on Monday at the ITV studios, because she wanted an interview for a new one-off series she was recording. Becky and I were ecstatic. We were struggling to believe it — but through the power of trust things were working out far, far beyond our imagination.

The day came for me to appear on *This Morning*. They sent a car to meet me at the station, paid my expenses — and then out of the blue Becky got a call to do Jury Service, so she could not come with me. Theresa came instead. Everyone at the studio was kind and friendly, making me feel at ease. I couldn't believe the amount of toast that they got through in the Green Room where we were joined with the other people due on the show. Instead of feeling nervous, I was enjoying myself. The few drops of the flower remedy I had been dropping on to my tongue since six that morning were working.

A preview shot of me was taken and make-up applied, and I was taken into the studio. Suddenly there was an announcement: Richard

Master Your Own Destiny

Hammond from *Top Gear* had had a serious car crash. There was a news flash, which naturally Philip Schofield and Fern Britton had to give. This only lasted a few minutes but they did this in the other half of the studio from where I was sitting comfortably with agony aunt Denise sitting beside me.

Then they casually walked over to me with my book in their hands, sat down and we just chatted. I found myself loving every minute. It surprised me how small the studio was but I concentrated on speaking and looking directly at Philip and Fern so as not to be distracted by the cameramen. Then my time on screen was over — but Theresa and I remained in the studio while they opened the phone lines for Denise to take some calls from viewers. So many people needed to hear about the happy ending to my own situation, and also to know that there was help for themselves out there.

Theresa and I went to lunch nearby, and I took a couple of phone calls from friends saying they had seen me on telly. Greta had been at the gym on a running machine, when suddenly she looked up and there I was on the huge screen. Other friends had been doing the ironing or having coffee when they were stopped in their tracks. I had told hardly anyone about the interview because I felt that the point was not to show off but to get my message across to the public.

This still left one puzzle to work out: I had been told that it would be *Richard & Judy* — so why was it *This Morning* when it became reality? Of course there *was* a connection: the time slot for *This Morning* is exactly where *Richard & Judy* had first started many years ago! This was also my first time on television, so the relevance was all the more powerful. Allowing and detaching from the end result is so important, because when you leave it to the Universe you get bigger and better results than you ever imagine.

Unfortunately Sharon Osborne had to cancel at the last minute because David Beckham had agreed to give an interview and of course I could not compete with him! But I didn't mind because I'd had such a wonderful experience being on *This Morning*. One thing was still missing however … an audience in the studio. I 'know' that will happen one day but I am not pushing it because it is part of the grand plan my helpers have for me.

It was also a great experience for Becky's CV. Since then she has managed to get more people on television, so there is another example of how trusting, having a faith in your project, brings amazing results. Obviously this will not happen to everyone but aiming high, keeping focused and putting in the hard work are all part of the process. If Becky and I had just sat back and not worked at it, maybe nothing would have happened. It has brought us both very valuable credibility.

A couple of months after this experience I was at Professional Speakers Association meeting for the start of a new year. Members were asked for inspiration about what we had each accomplished and learned. Of course I had to share my experience, which resulted in a big round of applause and inspiration for others that they could do the same.

Over the years I have shared how I did it with many colleagues, because I truly believe that what you give out you receive in return. It costs me nothing to share, other than a bit of my time. Imagination, following your gut instinct and stepping outside your comfort zone can bring many rewards both in business and in your personal life.

Point To Ponder

- What could you do to step outside your comfort zone and aim for a goal?
- What 'hook' can you think of that would work for you?
- Who do you think could help you, without breaking the bank?
- What thoughts and ideas won't leave you alone?
- What would be the ultimate success you could create for a project?

Hopefully you will have done your affirmations, worked out what you want and visualised it — but so often people don't really know what they want. They only *think* they do. Does the thought of what you want in life excite you? Does the idea of it wake you in the night because your mind won't lie still? Does your heart beat faster when you think about how to set about your goal in life, now that you know it is the right path for you?

But what if life is meant to be just as it already is? Things may be starting to unfold in your life already but you are wearing blinkers and can't see the road ahead. So, before we get to goal setting *for you*, here is an exercise to help you find your true purpose and passion. (If you already know what you want in life, skip this exercise and read on.)

Purpose and passion exercise

Take a sheet of paper or open a Word document on your computer, grab a cup of coffee or tea and put some music on. Then just write down every thought that means something to you in one word or short sentence. Write what you love, what inspires you, what you are good at... and keep writing. Let the thoughts and words flow. Carry on writing until you get to at least 150-200 words if not more. Add your strengths, the things you love doing, and your values until you get to a stage when you suddenly realise that you have a gut feeling deep inside.

Now stop writing. Go over the list and cross off the least important things. Get your juices flowing again and begin to feel the excitement that this exercise can bring; or it may make you cry. You will cry from deep emotion when something resonates with you. If you don't have one or other of these strong feelings then you haven't done this exercise properly.

Start all over again. Every job you have ever had; what were your strengths, what did it teach you? Your life experiences; what have they taught you? What hobbies are you good at? Can you begin to see a pattern running through your list? Imagine a pyramid and that your jobs and experiences are all leading you to the focus point at the top. You have learned those skills for a reason. What restricts you, or makes you feel enclosed? What do you hate or love doing the most? Keep asking yourself questions, so the list can go on and on.

This may take 20 minutes, as some people claim, or it may take 20 hours. If this exercise simply doesn't resonate with you, then work on the last exercise in Chapter Seven ('writing your epitaph'). It is a similar experience but by writing this all down it gives you a focus on your

> strengths and weaknesses, likes and dislikes, and you can then begin to recognise and go with your flow.

For those of you who already know what you want and are ready to set yourself some goals, there are many ways to do this. You can do it in one huge leap, or you can take one small step at a time.

Either way, it is important to focus and get a passion and purpose ignited; without that, it is hard to succeed. Your goal should scare you a little but it should excite you at the same time. A passion might be to accomplish a life-changing experience or a lifelong dream — but a small change could be just as influential and life-changing.

To summarise:

- Small steps are believable and therefore achievable.
- Every step you take brings you one step closer to where you want to be.
- Breaking down a goal into chunks makes it more manageable.
- You can break it down into monthly, weekly and even daily tasks.

Let's imagine that your goal is to get your current weight of 164 pounds down to 140 pounds. That goal of losing 24 pounds (or two stone) sounds a lot. Break it down and it sounds much better — what about two pounds a month for a year?

Or perhaps you want to save £5,000 in a year. That works out at £416 per month. Or you could call it £104.16 per week or even £13.60 per day. That sounds much more manageable than £416.66 per month!

You need to do what *you* feel is right, even if others mock or criticise you. By all means you should take advice and bounce ideas around with other people — but ultimately it must be your own decision to move in a certain direction.

There may be risks for you but your goals must be founded on reality, with realistic expectations, your skills and experience and the effort and preparations you are prepared to put in.

It's important to keep stretching and re-focusing your goals just as you are about to achieve them. You can nudge the goalpost just a little bit further, towards the next goal, so that it is just out of reach. Over time, you find you have been capable of attaining things you never thought you could. You need to keep moving the line further away — but still reachable. So many people attain their first goal and just look for the next thing, or give up if they come upon a hurdle.

This is important: you must write the goal in the present tense, as if it has already occurred. This will change your mindset. Instead of it just being a wish, you make it believable in your mind.

For example:

> I will build an extension to my house.
>
> I have built an extension to my house.

Notice the difference? When you read the first example it feels like a distant hope or wish that may happen some day. The second example will make you feel empowered that you have accomplished something. You can then visualise the house having its extensions and imagine what you are doing in the house! Belief is a powerful creative energy.

As you gain in confidence, taking each step at a time, you can look back after a while and see how far you have come. Many things in life will be unfolding already, so you need to start looking out for them, and not miss them. Are there significant things screaming at you, for example, that you love doing? Suddenly you begin to see that you've moved out of your comfort zone, you begin to feel really alive again.

All sorts of feelings and emotions emerge at this stage. It might include a buzz running through your whole body, if the change or goal is a big one. This is because, as you get nearer to achieving your goal, and get better at ignoring and proving wrong the small negative voice in your head that says 'you can't do that', you feel great. That little voice is nothing more than the self-talk you have got used to hearing.

Even a small change, whether in business or our personal life, can be the beginning of something much bigger. Whatever it is you want to achieve — whether it involves relationships, health, weight, career — by following your intuition, instincts and thoughts, by knowing that it can be done and is right for you, you are starting on the most magical journey.

If any of this feels uncomfortable, or if you feel at all uneasy, then it may just be wrong to pursue it at this time — or it could be something completely wrong. Maybe there are other things you should put in place first, before you can take all the necessary steps to get there. Sometimes obstacles need to be cleared from as deep a place as your subconscious. I know this from personal experience: my subconscious mind started re-living a past experience that I had thought I had already dealt with.

When I started this new business with Theresa, and we set ourselves brilliant goals and started working towards them, we were buzzing. Everything was going according to plan — and then one Friday night Theresa's husband Adonis suddenly died, aged just 39. The shock sent me straight back to when my husband had left me, more than ten years before. I honestly believed that I had dealt with all those feelings, and every thing else that went with that time, but obviously deep down I hadn't.

For three days I cried and cried. It all came back to me as if I were reliving all the emotions and fears. But then, just as suddenly as it came, when I realised what was happening, it flowed over and out of me, and I knew I had been cleansed.

Over the years this has happened to many of my friends — so I know that from personal experience, coaching and listening to others it can be a necessary process. It nearly always happens unexpectedly, or when you reach a crisis point and think: 'Where did *that* come from?'

But in order to move on, if something like this happens you do need to deal with it.

A friend and work colleague went through something similar recently: just when she had started a new business and was ecstatic about how well everything was flowing, out of the blue a thunderbolt from her childhood hit her hard. Again, she had believed deep down that she had worked out her emotions from the past … but then it was as if a weight she hadn't known she was bearing was lifted off her shoulders.

You don't have to let this sort of setback, or anything else, stop you. Focus, attitude and a deep desire are all you need. You can choose to let any negative thoughts or experiences go — because in the grand scheme of things you know in your subconscious mind or Higher Self that this is part of your pre-planned journey here on Earth.

Personal bolts from the Universe can happen too. I know because I've had a few of them! Relationships suddenly break down and a partner may walk out; you are made redundant or something else major happens. However, they can be a blessing in disguise. Devastation can also mean a complete change, ultimately for the better. Many new businesses result from people being made redundant. Many new marriages are the result of a previous failed relationship. It is natural occasionally to feel bitter at such times — but it is also a time to reflect.

What can you learn from this terrible thing that has happened? You have to be honest with yourself, and it is not always easy. You might need to see another person's point of view as well as your own. An experience like this can be a huge lesson — and believe it or not it can be a gift. When you release all these blocks it enables you to move on.

Each person reading this book will have a different goal or idea, and will achieve things at a different rate. It's not a race. There are no set rules. Follow your heart and your instincts will kick in. Outside circumstances will play a role, and they can be a distraction — but when you truly want something you need to get into the right mindset by raising your vision.

The Reverend Dr Martin Luther King junior said: 'Faith is taking the first step even when you don't see the whole staircase. Take the ladder of success one step at a time, by seeing each step, living each step and appreciating each step.'

You also need to realise that if you just send out thoughts to the Universe and *do* nothing — then you *get* nothing. Things don't mysteriously appear in your life without a bit of effort! Don't worry if you don't have all the resources or education you need yet. Just start moving and your guidance will help you find the solutions you need.

So, how do you move on and achieve your goal? At the back of this book, I have some helpful lists which you can photocopy and write on. They include actions to be taken each day and month. Here is a brief list to start with:

1. Recognise whether your goal is an *intention* or just something you *want*. These are different: an *intention* will always materialise because the desire behind it adds a driving force.

2. Write down everything you want to achieve — but be realistic. If it is not realistic it will never happen.

3. Begin to see yourself achieving the end result.

4. Know that there may be hiccups along the way but don't let them turn into negative excuses to give up on your goal.

5. Keep a book or a Dictaphone beside you at all times, for when ideas and inspirations pop into your head. You don't always remember them later.

6. Think of a reward you can give yourself when you have achieved certain steps.

7. Write down the first few steps that you need to take, and then all the other steps as you go along. Or, if you already know exactly what you want, then set all the goals down.

8. Write down how you will feel in one year's time.

9. If it is a personal goal, such as finding a new partner, consider where can you go, what club can you join, what can you learn which could introduce you to someone like-minded. A hobby or a new interest can be a brilliant way to move on.

10. If the goal is a new business, do all of the above but start networking with others to learn and grab all the information you can.

11. Ask others for advice but always follow your own gut instincts and heart.

12. Consider collaborating with others who have different skills to your own.

13. Think about whether you need to learn new skills.

14. Last but not least, ask the Universe for help. Often people are afraid to ask or don't know how. When your spirit guides see that you are committed and you are taking action on your

goals, they will back you with new opportunities beyond your dreams. They cannot move into action on your behalf until you do. Keep taking action and never allow doubt to creep in and you will be rewarded. In a later chapter more will be revealed!

Secrets for successful people:
- Find new opportunities that resonate with you.
- Love what you do and put your heart and soul into it.
- Realise that fear is not real if you are on the right path and it feels right.
- Find *lessons* instead of seeing only *problems*.
- Stay focused and don't let fear limit you.
- Keep stretching yourself just that little bit further.
- Persist: successful people are no cleverer than you. They just keep at it.
- Give to others; they will give back to you.
- Develop a positive attitude: it is the driving force.
- Be ambitious and ask the right questions. Ask for help if need be.
- Know what you want and deal with problems as and when they arise.
- Keep learning.
- Understand the importance of discipline and self-control.
- Time management and a happy work-life balance are important.
- Learn to relax, enjoy what you have already in life, and have some fun on the journey.

Each opportunity that has come my way has not always turned out as I expected. Many have exceeded my expectations but one or two have sent me on a huge learning curve. Every time, I have followed my intuition.

Olympia, London

I was asked to give two different talks at Olympia for the Retirement Show, and I was over the moon. To be asked to talk at such a huge event was at the time nerve-wracking but I was certainly up for the challenge. I had changed my whole life very near to retiring age; if I could do it I was sure others could too. But it didn't turn out quite as expected.

My friend Lesley Greenwood agreed to come with me on the first day. I had done all the necessary preparation, prepared my speech and was confident that it would be fun. What I didn't realise was that as it was a working day, the only attendees would be pensioners themselves, who had already retired — some of them many years ago and now in their eighties and nineties. They had all come because admission was free, and of course they got free travel, so it would be a great day out for them. How was I going to inspire them to do something exciting with their retirement and keep the audience from falling asleep in front of me?

Thinking on my feet, I hastily re-cast my whole message — and it ended up as a huge success. I told them a little about myself and what I had achieved, along with some funny stories. Then I found a few members of the audience who had done amazing things too, and who were willing to share their experiences.

One lady, well into her eighties had been a nurse; she had travelled all over the world on her own after her husband died. Another lady, in her seventies, had spent three months in South America doing voluntary work in an orphanage, and was going to India in a few months' time to do the same there. Talking to her afterwards, she revealed she was a titled lady — but you would never have known it. She said that to give in to her loneliness after her husband died would have been awful, and she loved helping others who gave her so much more back. She said the spiritual journey she was now embarking on was more rewarding than anything she had ever done.

The next day, a friend Mandy came with me. I enjoyed it even more because I could relate to the audience being vibrant and closer to my own age! They had been working the day before, so I gave a talk on writing and marketing a book which was a huge success. Many of the audience had been writing secretly for years, or writing was going to be their new venture, and they asked me for more details. This experience really taught me that, as a speaker or in any other profession, you have to be adaptable.

Many people have helped me in my vision to succeed. I am grateful to them all and Max, the two Lesley's, Becky, Margaret, Theresa, Mark and Nick have been hugely instrumental for various reasons. However, there is one other person who is an example of how willing people are to share with each other. I am not sure that all professions are as open or willing; some can be cut-throat and back-stabbing. Still, I have always believed that what you give out you receive in return.

At the beginning of my speaking career I met Alan Stevens, the media coach, who has recently served as President of the Professional Speakers Association. He gave me some brief advice on working with the media, because I had planted the seed out to the Universe that I wanted to appear on television. Of course, as you now know, my wish was to be granted.

When I next bumped into him I told him about my success and he was thrilled for me. We got chatting and I mentioned that my next obstacle was finding my niche. He told me that if I bought him a tuna melt and a coffee he would be all ears.

Alan is a busy man but we arranged a date and time and I drove over to where he lives. We chatted in a local restaurant for two and a half hours. He gave me one of my *Aha!* ideas, which was to use a key in my talks as I am often a catalyst for others to open their own doors. This kick-started some inspiration and cleared a few blocks. That little idea just grew and grew on my way home and ignited my passion even more.

I arranged for Waitrose to deliver some champagne to him as a thank you, because I was grateful for the time he had given up for me. The price of a tuna melt and coffee just didn't seem enough. (So thank you again, Alan, as many people have told me that I often pop into their head when they are turning their own key!)

When you are in a profession or job that inspires you, it is so much easier to inspire others. Even when you work in a large organisation for someone else, you can keep challenging yourself, learning new skills or just fulfilling the role as it suits you. We don't all need to be in dead-end jobs. You can climb the ladder wherever you are working — but if you don't feel fulfilled in any way then perhaps it is time to step outside your comfort zone and look for something else. Scary as it might seem to contemplate a move, that very job could be strangling you. Nothing has to be drastic — you can take your time and look out for something which *would* excite you.

I recently coached a client called Frank, who hated his job in the City. He was a high flyer in administration but it was eating away at him. It was starting to affect his relationship at home, as every night he was full of anger which he couldn't let go. He had a young family and his wife was expecting another baby, and he couldn't leave the job because it paid the bills. We looked at his various options and he rejected every one of them. Suddenly my guides asked me to ask him about a silly idea he'd a few weeks ago. He stopped in his tracks and said: 'How did you know that?' I asked: 'What feelings do you get when you drive past the local prison? Fancy working as a Prison Officer?'

Suddenly his passion was ignited. His instinct was telling him something every time he passed that prison but it scared him and he didn't understand what it meant. What I didn't know was that ten years earlier he had been in the armed forces, and missed the comradeship and structure. He even missed the uniform.

Armed with his true mission, he was now like a new man. Suddenly he knew what he wanted to do. It will take time, I am sure, for this to materialise but as he said: 'Just having something to aim for is like a huge weight being lifted off my shoulders.' At the time of writing this he has applied for an application form, been to various job agencies in his spare time, and got out all his old Army records. He is determined to do this. The salary will be less but the pressure is off and his wife is going to work part-time to help out.

What he had not known is that she was thinking of doing this anyway. She hadn't wanted to tell him because he was so angry all the time. Honest conversations can really work.

Let's recap...

STEP 1 — Meditate every day and keep a diary.

STEP 2 — Let go of fears, core conditioning and resistance.

STEP 3 — Practise visualisation and follow your instincts, hunches and sudden ideas.

STEP 4 — Believe in yourself.

STEP 5 — Rise to a challenge. Overcome obstacles and have some fun.

STEP 6 — Your life has a blueprint so let your life unfold as it should be.

STEP 7 — Set your own goals and don't be frightened to step outside your comfort zone. Make your goals realistic but they must have an end result.

So far I have given you hints, tips, ideas, suggestions and lots of information. You could stop here, and you will have already gained a lot from this book.

However, to learn and understand much more about how life works and get a good overall picture of how to create your own success, you may want to delve a little deeper by reading the next few chapters.

But let me ask you something first: is something missing in your life, and you are not sure what it is? Are you someone who has all the material trappings but still feels empty inside?

Have you started to have a curious interest in the concept there may be more to life than just this? Or have you started to experience some wonderful sensations or seen visions? Are you simply becoming open to the idea that there might be someone or something out there in the Universe? Do you want to learn more?

Then please read on.

Nurture Your Own Goals

Chapter Eight

Spiritual extras

*To hear the Voice of Silence is to understand that
from within comes the only true guidance.*
— *John Algeo*

We are all one

At the very beginning of my spiritual journey, when I was seeing colours and pictures, hearing music and words, it gave me such a blissful feeling that in some ways I never felt alone. I was being looked after by my 'helpers' which in itself was a fantastic experience. And then other events and experiences started to happen which made this all the more powerful. I wanted to learn more.

In the fifteen years that followed, I have learned and experienced such a lot which I want to share with you. This has helped me to understand that there is far more to life than I realised. I want to help you understand, as I have, that there is a true reason we are enrolled in the School of the Universe.

We are all spiritual beings, having a human experience, and I want to share with you how I know this to be true.

I am not going to go into every scientific detail about all the areas I am going to cover, because it's more important to understand this in simple terms. I would like to give you an overall picture of what life is all about — but I am only writing about *my* experiences and what *I* understand. I could never teach you this; I can only guide and advise. It is all highly personal, different for everyone. You have to feel some of this within.

There are many people out there with different ideas, theories and experiences. That is fantastic because it means the world is waking up to a much richer life. If you want to learn more at a later stage about any aspect that you have read about in this book, I will be delighted.

That would mean I have whetted your appetite to learn more — and that is exactly what this book is about!

Numerous subjects, ideas and even spiritual and scientific findings are being uncovered every day. To keep up with it all would be impossible and I would not be able to cover everything. I have had to leave out some subjects because they would warrant a whole book on their own. However, in the Appendices at the end of this book I have compiled a list of suggested reading that will allow you to delve into any of these at a later stage if you wish.

What I will give you is a brief outline which is just *my* theory of what I call 'how life works'. Don't forget we are each masters of our own destiny; what resonates with one person may be different to another.

Some of you reading this will have a strong religious belief. I want to make sure there is no confusion here, and hopefully no offence taken, because what is in this book has nothing to do with any religion. To me, and to many others, spirituality is much more about you as a person, getting in touch with the inner you, and empowering you to find the peace and love you have been seeking. For those of you who are spiritual and *not religious*, my words will speak to your soul. We are all one, and I believe come from the same source — it's just a different story.

The belief of the true beauty within ourselves is what matters to me, not who you believe in.

My understanding

Before all this spiritual stuff happened, I had no idea that many people in my life had been with me before in a past life and were part of my soul family; I just accepted them for who they were. I never questioned how they had come to be in my life. After my parents died I wrote my first book, *Before I Get Old and Wrinkly*, as I realised that I hadn't really known them as people. They somehow were just my parents … yet there is far more to it than just that!

I have many friends, some of whom I have known for many years, since we were teenagers. As my life has opened up I have made lots of new friends too. These new friends have come into my life, enabling me to grow as my interests have changed, since the time when I was married.

My family has also grown. One of my most magical experiences was when I was at the birth of my first granddaughter. My daughter had split up with her partner of a year, just two weeks before she found out she was pregnant; she chose to be a single parent and the whole family supported her in that decision. Two weeks prior to her due date, she was rushed into hospital for an emergency caesarean section. I received a frantic phone call to say could I please hurry to the hospital because my granddaughter's father could not be there.

Anni was gowned up and had been given an epidural and covered in green sheets so we could not see anything. I sat at the end of the operating table, holding and stroking her head, not knowing what else to do. The surgeons and nurses were running around the room … and then suddenly the surgeon looked straight at me and passed this tiny precious gift of a life, covered in blood and with the cord still attached, into my hands. I held her to my daughter's face. Suddenly I saw this little bundle's nostrils pop open and the surgeon said to me: 'You have just witnessed your granddaughter's first breath.'

Then her little ears popped out, from being stuck against her head, and it was one of the most magical moments in my entire life. To watch the miracle of a baby being born is a joy beyond words. My daughter and I both burst into tears, as she had so wanted a girl. Then they took the baby away and cleaned her up before handing her properly to her mother.

I had two children of my own. But the truth is, when you give birth, you are utterly exhausted. A new mother does of course feel the joy and love instantly — but this was different. My daughter and granddaughter came to live with me for six weeks, as she couldn't lift or do anything herself; I began to see my first grandchild as one of my own. Over the next few years they were both constantly in my life and my house but I had no idea just how special to me this little girl was going to be.

As a spiritual Circle we had decided to spend a weekend as a group in Glastonbury. I was still learning quickly, and was excited about visiting this famous place. I somehow knew deep inside that this trip was going to be special; I didn't realise how significant until I returned home.

A silver thread to a member of my soul family

I had promised my granddaughter that I would bring her back a small present from Glastonbury. It's not really the place to buy anything small for children — but in a book shop they had some beanbag animals for sale, which would fit the bill. So, I went to a little basket that had a yellow beanbag duck in it. Just right, I thought, as her favourite bedtime story is about a duck which she called the Duck Duck book.

When I took this duck to the lady at the counter she said to me: 'Do you want *this* duck? It is a very special duck as it only has one eye.' I thought about it, and decided to get another one from the shelf; the faulty one might have been cheaper, but would my granddaughter notice? Thinking nothing more of it, I packed it in my overnight bag, and after another long journey, arrived home.

My granddaughter, who was three years old at the time, came running to open the door. I said: 'If you would like to look in my bag you will find a little present.' The most amazing thing happened. She found the brown paper bag and looked inside, and proceeded to take out the beanbag duck. She then said to me: 'Nanny, why didn't you buy me that *special duck*? That was the one I wanted.'

I and everyone else were speechless. We could not believe what she had just said. How could she know about the little duck more than 200 miles away, that I had picked up just a few hours earlier?

That was an extremely powerful experience. I have since discovered that my granddaughter and I have a very special spiritual bond that can never be broken; she is part of my soul family, even a soul mate, which I will explain a little further on. I am sure she will develop her own psychic abilities later in life. As a child she played for hours with her 'special friends' and always felt protected by a toy angel that I gave her for her bedroom.

One of my other grandchildren used to talk to my Dad, and pointed him out to me on numerous occasions from one of my pictures by my kitchen table. My Dad had died long before my grandson was born, and he used to say that 'James' came and chatted to him at night time. When he was at school he said that James helped him in the playground, and he said it in such a convincing way I never disbelieved him. As he has got older he has stopped mentioning James and I am not pushing it.

Many children have 'special friends' whom they see and actually talk to, because children are far more connected than adults to the source of where they have come from. I don't think anyone truly knows whether babies do see spirit — but if you watch carefully, very small children will often follow with their eyes something or someone you cannot see. They will even laugh at something for no apparent reason; maybe they *are* seeing someone.

There are also many children who suddenly start to talk in a completely different language. Others can lead you to a place they 'know' already. They can describe details that no-one can explain, and when investigated they have been proved right. I think there has to be something in this.

Has anything like this happened to you?

- You remember having your own 'special' friends.
- You have felt uneasy when in a house or a place.
- You felt inexplicably uneasy about something and were later proved correct.
- Life has suddenly become more peaceful as if you have a deep inner knowing.
- You have 'heard' a little voice at the back of your head.
- You have an inner voice that gives you helpful advice but are not sure where it comes from.
- You have sudden flashes of visions but don't understand what they mean.
- You 'talk' to spirit guides or Angels and sense they are listening, even though you are apparently alone.
- You feel occasional tingles, smell something strange or feel a

breath of air somewhere on you, maybe on your face.
- You sensed that something was going to happen and it did.
- You have always felt 'different' and you are not sure why.

I used to feel 'different' when I was younger and I had no idea why. I even told my friends that I had been adopted because no-one in my family could understand some of the things I talked about. I had such a deep sense of 'inner-knowing' that I could not explain, that had always been with me. Some of my friends and colleagues have been brought up in a family where this was the 'norm' — but many others have been what I call 'awakened' any time from their mid-thirties onwards.

For many this has happened at a crisis point. For others it was a natural progression stemming from a curiosity. We can all learn, if we wish, to open our psychic ability. It can be an amazing help with guidance but is not necessarily for everyone. Some people search their whole life long to experience this beautiful gift and never find it. There are others who take it too far, and live in what I call La-La Land!

A spiritual growth is rarely a sudden awareness, and it doesn't happen automatically; it's a gradual process. It comes through self-awareness, and it takes effort and deep thought, to get a clear vision of your purpose in life and feel serenity. However, as you begin this journey, your true enlightenment will speak for itself. You will demonstrate it in your actions and in the very essence of how you are. You will begin to radiate a light around yourself; if you have to *tell* people you are living a spiritual life, then you are probably not. True spiritual growth will be when people say: 'There is just something about them that I can't put my finger on — but somehow they are beautiful.' This happens when you begin to feel inner peace.

As I said earlier, living a more spiritual life is not just about opening yourself to your guides. It is more about living as the authentic *you*. Following your gut instinct and intuition is one of the most important ways that your guides and spiritual helpers can communicate with you through your Higher Self. If you can imagine a big power surrounding you, that you know is there but that you can't see, then that is a wonderful way to start to understand this. Your helpers, or this bigger power, come through when you are in dream state, meditation and through your intuition — or, for the real psychic stuff, through your 'third eye', which is in the middle of your forehead, between your eyebrows.

This is an area which fascinates me. I could not understand how the pictures I could see were beamed down to me, or even where they were coming from. And what did this powerful connection to my granddaughter mean?

My new-found spiritual friends recommended I read a couple of books, and I do find this the best way to understand some of the more in depth explanations. So, off I went to a bookshop again. Over the next few years I read many books. The three most influential for helping me understand some of my experiences are: *Many Lives, Many Masters* by Dr Brian Weiss; *Journey of Souls* by Michael Newton; and *Ask and It is Given* by Esther and Jerry Hicks.

The first, *Many Lives, Many Masters*, is by prominent American psychiatrist and scientist Dr Brian Weiss. Many years ago he accidentally regressed one of his patients into a past life. Over a period of time, the woman continued to go back into different lives whilst under hypnosis; he started to record the meetings because this past life regression started to cure her psychiatric disorder. He wanted to collect evidence that we *all* have been here on planet Earth before, in a past life. Sometimes many lifetimes were recorded, and he believes that most of us will come back again too; this made sense to me. It took him four years to disclose his findings because he was afraid of what his colleagues would say — but by then he had the evidence which he could no longer ignore.

Why would we be here on Earth if there wasn't a purpose? And where did we come from? Surely we can't all have come from nowhere, and then just disappear into nothing? To me, people are too precious. I simply could never understand why some people assume that there is nothing more to themselves than just *this* existence.

The sceptics I have spoken to can never give me an explanation for this, and many of them are quite happy about that. But I find it sad that they don't seem to have much depth to their lives. Many of them feel that only a scientific explanation will justify them even *thinking* about this. Dr Weiss is one of many who are realising the truth behind this concept. People are beginning to awaken to a new reality, including scientists themselves!

Many people fear death because they don't understand or know anything about this beautiful concept. I think these fears may stem from the pain you may feel at the time of your death due to a possible illness, and many people worry that they may have a feeling of nothingness afterwards. But the good news is that we do live on after death.

Some regard even talking about death as off limits, presumably on the grounds that if they don't think about it, it won't happen! Birth and death are the two certainties in life. Your soul is well prepared for death; it knows it will not be destroyed because it is just going home. We all come from the same source (our birth) and will go back to the same source (our death) and many describe that as a feeling of going home, a joyous event.

You leave your physical body behind but the main essence of you — your soul — goes home. You leave all your mental and physical pain behind, and as the expression says: 'You can't take it with you when you are gone' — meaning all the material things we accumulate.

You fear death, I am sure, because of leaving behind your loved ones; also your loved ones don't want to let you go either. But we are never really far apart, because in the spirit world we can look after and watch over our loved ones. And we will be reunited one day.

Your soul never dies; it merely moves to a different layer of consciousness. We are all eternal. Death is not darkness, but light. Your soul returns to the light.

You return home to your soul family (see below) which is now understood to be nothing other than a higher level of consciousness, or the first level in the Astral Plane — and from everything I have read, it is blissful. There are many other, higher levels which I will explain later, where our guides, masters and Angels hop about from one realm to the other. I have to say it sounds like fun 'up there' — but we will learn more about that shortly.

We are all made from *energy*. Your soul, the core of your being, comes with you life after life — but you take on a different persona and body in each life time. We have all lived as male and female previously, and learned many things in each lifetime.

Sometimes you come back to teach what you have learned. You may have experienced something in a previous life, which affects you in this lifetime. For example, many people who have a fear of water have found, in a past life regression session under hypnosis, that they drowned in a previous life. Once this block is cleared, their fear of water disappears.

Apparently, we choose to return to Earth. The reason for doing this varies from person to person — but you agree with your spiritual Masters and your guides, before you come here, what it is you need to learn or experience. Some come to teach, others to learn to be loved or how to deal with an emotion such as anger, jealousy or a separation. Despite what you may have been led to believe, it isn't always something major. Some may have many lessons, others just one or two. Often, you have experiences which are simply 'triggers' reminding you in your subconscious mind that you are on the right path.

We each have free will and can choose to lead a completely different life if we want to. There is no right or wrong way to lead your life — but hopefully for your spiritual growth you are being the authentic *you.*

This can be hard to understand ... but many people's lives are taken from them at an early age. That is part of their destiny. For whatever reason, their time on Earth has been completed. A friend of mine, Sheila, always said she never wanted to grow old. She had a sort of inner-knowing that she was not meant to be here to live through old age, and she died in a car crash at the age of fifty. Her family and friends will never know why, but she does; as do others when they pass over to the higher realms.

Your Higher Self knows what you need to achieve in this lifetime. By connecting to it, you can access your life's plan. As we discussed earlier, you can access this through meditation, dreams and intuition. Your spiritual helpers and Angels just remind you and give you gentle nudges with guidance, and can help you accelerate your personal and spiritual growth.

Many people continue a pattern to their lives which they may have experienced in a past life. Or they may have come here to experience it for the first time — for example abuse or suffering. Remember we talked about *The Boy Whose Skin Fell Off?* He understood this concept brilliantly. Once this is recognised and the patterns change, you have dealt with your lesson and it will not happen again in this lifetime — or even in a future lifetime — unless you let it happen.

Is this *karma*, as some people say? Theories about this differ, and the saying *What comes around goes around* may be true. However, if you do horrible things or experience trauma, could this be related to something in your past? Many 'channelled' books say that this is not always the case, because karma is also an opportunity to learn and to practise love and forgiveness. Karma is also an opportunity for atonement; to wipe the slate clean and make things up with those you have wronged in the past.

Karma is about love and knowledge, and is mentioned in nearly all religions, so you must remember that we are all responsible for our own actions.

Soul families

Soul families make perfect sense to me because sometimes you just *know* someone from the depth of their soul; you have a much closer deeper bond than with others, even your blood relations. Many people have looked into someone's eyes (the windows of the soul, remember) and had a complete understanding that this person is going to be special to them; and they are.

You choose your parents before you come into this world because of what they can teach you. They are usually souls with whom you have interacted in prior lifetimes. They are not from your soul family — but many of your close relations, partners or siblings can be.

Close friends with whom you have a deep friendship and love can often be someone you have had a relationship in a past life. They may even be from your soul family. In previous lives you may have played the role of a child, a brother or sister or partner or friend, because the roles are changed for the lessons you need to learn and experience for whatever is necessary. Sometimes you come back with the same souls time and time again because you need to learn or master something which you may not have done in that lifetime.

To help you understand this more clearly, the best description I can show you is in the drawing.

Master Your Own Destiny

Your Soul Tree

Imagine all your soul family (as souls) residing in the trunk of a tree. Trees have many branches, and each branch has its own soul family. Often the people you connect with here on Earth are from one of your branches. You can have a strong connection with a person because you have pre-planned that you shall meet, for whatever reason.

Every person in your own soul family will be someone very special to you. We can each have more than one soul mate because all families have a different number of souls. It is said that each soul family is here on Earth working on something united, and this will be different for each group. Each group will be made up of a different number of souls.

Soul relationships can be in a husband/wife relationship, siblings, co-workers, close friends or other relationships — but a soul mate is like the echo of yourself. They are often mother/daughter, father/son, husband/wife. You connect in each lifetime with the same soul group; however you meet as a different person with a different relationship, which is something you need for our spiritual growth.

There are many soul groups in the astral planes. You will never have a connection to most of them because you will have no need.

When you do connect with someone, it can sometimes feel like an instant rapport; the world suddenly feels much smaller. Such people are from a closer group to yours than some of the other people with whom you've connected in everyday life.

If you have children you will know by now that each child was on a different path right from birth! You can bring them all up in exactly the same way but as they get older (or even at a quite a young age) they can go in a completely different direction. Children each have a unique personality from birth. Look closely and you will see that they are actually following their own individual journey — just as you have done. They have chosen you as parents for what you can teach them, and that's why you should not restrict their growth by insisting they do as you say with their life. They have their own life to lead and you are merely providing guidance.

There are many kinds of relationship including *karmic*, *soul mates* and *twin flames* (which are very special indeed).

Twin flames were created together at the beginning of time and share a unique destiny. Aeons ago, you and your twin flame were created in the image of God from out of the same cosmic sphere of consciousness — two flames of spirit, male and female, plus and minus in polarity. The two of you share the same cosmic blueprint that is not duplicated anywhere else in the cosmos. Your twin flame is your true 'other half'. To meet your twin flame, all karma must be balanced.

Soul mate relationship is probably the one that most people want in their life but you can have more than one. Your soul mate is the one who makes life come alive; the bond is so close, you feel that the two of you are one but you each have your own twin flame.

A karmic relationship, which is the most common union, happens when you are drawn together for the balancing of mutual karma. All relationships have to be worked at and most relationships in life are not free from hard times and conflict; when you work through these issues, you grow and evolve.

There are many fascinating books on this subject. This brief outline should have helped you to understand more about what I call 'how life works' and why you have some of the relationships in your life, so you can appreciate them more in the bond you have.

Don't just take people in your life for granted. They are special — *everyone* is — and they are in your life for a reason.

If you are a non-believer, you might ask yourself just why you should suddenly appear here on Earth, live your life and then disappear in a puff of smoke; there is always a reason and it was your own choice. Whoever you meet in any relationship, even just a friend or colleague, enjoy their company and you will teach each other something special.

Life after death

What happens after you die is not a mystery. Because your soul is of the Universe, you return there. Since your physical body belongs to the Earth, when you pass on, your body stays here. Because everything is energy, all things gravitate towards the same energy. While you are alive, because as matter you are *heavy*, gravity keeps you grounded. This is one way to explain life after death: there *is* no death. Your soul continues on a spiritual journey.

I would like to share with you a couple of experiences, to help you see that there really is no death. We merely pass onto a higher dimension, still connected, and we can still communicate with each other because we are all made up of the same energy. We do this through our open psychic centre, or telepathically through our thoughts and intuition (which I talked about earlier). There is nothing to fear.

This was demonstrated for me in an amazing but very sad experience: the sudden death of my friend Theresa's husband Adonis. It was a terrible shock and a tragedy to us all, and also was the catalyst for bringing up painful emotions I thought I had buried years before when my husband left me.

A few days after Adonis's death, a dozen of our spiritual Circle members held a Healing Circle for Theresa but not all of us could make it. One of our missing members, Anthony, came through telepathically to my psychic centre and asked me to say that he wished to be remembered; he was there with us tonight and wanted to send his love to Theresa. I passed on this message, which we all thought strange because he was one of the people not present. He had always loved being part of the Circle but had not attended for some time.

Sharon picked up on this because she had been concerned about him for a while. The very next day she went with a friend to his house, only to find that he had passed away in his sleep in his bed, a few days previously. So he had been with us ... in *spirit*.

I am not a medium. That's probably why Anthony chose me to connect with, because it was not the sort of thing I would normally have picked up on, let alone conveyed.

A few months later I was to have another experience which horrified me so much that I have asked my unseen 'helpers' for it never to happen again.

Adonis's death was sudden and horrific. The post mortem stated that he had died of a heart attack but to Theresa that didn't ring true; she was going through turmoil trying to work things out. He'd died at home in her arms after a horrific attack, too quickly for him to be able to tell her what was happening.

He had previously visited a dentist to have a wisdom tooth out — but, being a man, had taken some painkillers before he got there. The dentist then gave him some more, and Adonis's ulcer burst, contributing at least partly to a heart attack. How do I know this? Because I relived it at midnight one night!

I felt all the acid in my body come up into my throat; I was gagging and I thought I was going to die. Thankfully it subsided as quickly as it happened — but for those few moments it was a living hell.

Why Adonis and Anthony chose me to experience these events I am not sure; perhaps because people know I don't make things up. Or it could be that I am to experience *everything* … because lots of different things have started to happen to me, which I do want to learn more about. My knowledge on some of these subjects is limited at the moment — but I love learning.

One of the things I have started to do, with no idea how I do it, is to talk to other people telepathically while I'm asleep. Friends have received information that way, and a few have woken in the morning expecting to find me in their home!

I have also managed to do a couple of Past Life Regressions on myself and have jumped back in time. Once, I found myself in a castle in Scotland during the eighteenth century and was walking down a grand staircase. By contrast, I have also seen myself as a nurse in the trenches in the Crimean War. I could physically feel, smell and see my surroundings. My most recent regression was as a 1920s or 1930s debutante lady, dressed in a jade green silk dress and hat with a tiny eighteen-inch waist. It was a very posh 'do' and I was probably around the age of my late thirties, so I must have died quite young as that was not that long ago in objective time.

People who have died are merely living in a different dimension to you and me. We will meet them again when we ourselves pass over as a soul. Michael Newton, in his book *Journey of Souls*, has done pioneering research on the subject of what happens when you return home.

When you return 'home', you (your soul) are met (in general) by your guides and your soul groups, and all of you are surrounded with pure love. They appear as beings of light, made up of vibrant energy far more powerful than you can imagine. You go through a process of de-layering and healing — otherwise you would have difficulty in connecting to this higher vibration and light. Many people who have had near death experiences talk about this light.

We all have had many lifetimes and we choose to return to Earth as part of our spiritual growth. You might choose instead to go to other dimensions; many people say this physical Universe is only one of a multitude of Universes, all of them foreign to human concept. I find this believable: why should we be the only beings in this *Multiverse*?

As I understand it, when you return to Earth some of your energy is left behind with your surviving soul group, for you to connect with when you rejoin them again after a death. I believe this is because that is where your Higher Self is, and what you connect to sometimes via the psychic connection. Communication with each other, and with you, is made via thoughts telepathically relayed; they can take on any form they want if they wish to communicate with you. That is why you sometimes see *spirit* in physical form — because that is what you would recognise.

If you can imagine Angels with wings, then that is what you see (if you are lucky enough). They are far more advanced than you or I will ever be. In the last few decades our consciousness and vibration on Earth have risen and we have become more advanced. That is why this whole new stronger connection is happening around the globe as we become closer.

This is the part that interests me; how I could see all these pictures like a mini-film? The answer seems to be that they are made up of energy too. They are transmitted via light-images, thought-impulses or thermal and electromagnetic images, and one day you are going to see these too!

At some stage you seek to review the life that you have just lived; usually you do this with your guide, and you may do it in a number of ways. You might choose to go to a library of life books; on opening your own book it comes alive and enables you as a soul to watch a film of all the details of your life. Alternatively, you might review your life telepathically, or relive it. I don't fully understand how you do that yet but Michael Newton does explain it well in his book.

Whichever theory is the right one, to know that the pictures that are beamed down to me in a form of energy is astounding. So, what I see is in the same form as when I will be reviewing my life — but it takes our guides and Angels much concentration to send this down to the Earth plane.

I have also read that they can 'push' us with this powerful energy in a particular direction. This may account for what I can only describe as 'arranged meetings' — the ones that happen out of the blue. In the many books I've read there are several theories as to whether it is my Angels or my guides who are sending these messages. To me it doesn't matter. Either way, it's a privilege and I love receiving them.

Perhaps one day science will discover how powerful this energy is or how it is made up. Personally, I suspect you will only know when you return home.

Our guides, Angels and Masters

Who are these unseen helpers with whom I've had so many conversations over the past fifteen years? I do talk to my own Higher Self in the collective universal consciousness — but you have other helpers too, who can give you extra help, guidance and support. The extra dimension they bring can help you overcome your limiting beliefs.

When you are born, everyone is allocated a guide and a guardian angel who are with you at all times; they never intrude in your life and will only help if you ask. They are never judgmental but can show you simple ways to make life easier. They see the whole bigger picture of your life, and know you far better than you know yourself. Let me explain.

Your guide may be a loved one who has left this world and comes back every now and then to keep an eye on you. More usually, a guide might be a wiser spirit who has lived on Earth but has chosen to help you from another realm. A guide will usually appear to you as someone coming from a civilisation with centuries of history, such as a Tibetan monk, an American Indian, someone from ancient China or Egypt. Often their technology will have been in some ways ahead of our own, such as that of the ancient Mayans.

Different guides may come into your life at various times when you need a particular support or guidance; the same guide will not be with you throughout life. Learning to talk to your guide allows you to receive far more information than you can through signs alone.

There are also Masters — sometimes known as Elders, Higher Ones, Wise Ones or Masters of Light. They are spirits that have evolved beyond the need to incarnate; they are very special and occasionally they guide you, too. Normally they oversee your general guides in the higher realms, and it is a very special privilege for a Master to come into your life. He or she will surround you with a pure high vibrational energy, very different to your normal guide. They are masters of all knowledge.

Your guardian angel never changes. He or she will be with you throughout your life — but other Angels come in and go out again at any particular time. Angels are a much higher and finer vibrational pure energy than a guide. That is why you feel and see them differently. They are a much *lighter* energy which you can sometimes feel touching you with a tingle, a smell or just a little gentle sensation on your face or a particular part of your body. You may feel a small breeze, or see petals or feathers, and this all comes from Angels.

Angels and guides will never harm you. If you have a feeling that something doesn't feel right, then this is not from your spiritual helpers. Angels are messengers of light that have never lived on Earth — but they are fun and they want you to share with them the lighter side of life. Some people, when they feel Angels around them, just want to giggle. Angels are healers and perform miracles, and are sometimes known as the *cosmic connectors*.

There are of course higher beings of light known as *archangels*, the best-known being Archangels Michael, Gabriel, Uriel, Rapheal, Zadkiel, Chamuel, and Jophiel — each with a special role to play, healing the Universe and you and me. Angels were the chorus that sang to me when I heard the music in my ear. (See also Appendix B on Angel forums.)

One of the places we visited in Glastonbury was the Chalice Well, a beautiful spiritual garden open to everyone. It has a natural healing well whose waters are known to have healing powers, and it is visited by people from all over the world.

It is not a big garden, yet the feelings you get when you are there are beautiful and serene. Each of us drifted off to do our own thing. For some of us this was to be a meditation; for others it was just to connect our own thoughts and surroundings.

I found myself sitting on a seat by the well itself; I closed my eyes and just *sat*. After a few minutes, I began to see gorgeous colours swirling in front of my closed eyes, getting stronger and stronger. The colours I was seeing were all of nature. All the browns, greens, yellows, gold and rust, were like the autumn shades of leaves all blowing in front of me, all mixed into one. It was like a peacock's fanned tail but in different colours. Then, I saw all the colours of the rainbow, and the most beautiful blue, and then all the garden colours again, flowing in front of me. They were all surrounded by a wonderful white light, and so was I. We were one.

At the same time, I could feel someone wrapping their arms around me and hugging me tightly — but very gently — and my whole body was tingling. I couldn't move. I sat perfectly still, enjoying this beautiful feeling. It was the most peaceful experience I have ever had. I know I was being bathed in divine love and it was indescribable. I must have sat there for about half an hour, enjoying and embracing every moment… and then reluctantly and slowly I opened my eyes, to see Cathy our Circle leader standing in front of me in amazement: she had just witnessed a Messenger of Light standing behind me. I could not speak. Tears just ran down my face, and words were not needed.

Cathy and I hugged each other. There was no other way to express what we had both just experienced. Cathy has been surrounded by this sort of thing all of her life — but even she had never seen anything so beautiful and we both felt privileged, humble. To this day, it still brings tears to my eyes when I talk about it. I feel very special and privileged to have been chosen to receive such a wonderful, intensely loving experience

Quite a few of my friends have been touched by Angels or guides and had similar experiences, or have visited the spiritual or Angelic realms during a deep meditation. But one friend, Malcolm, had a completely different experience which neither I nor any of my friends can explain.

Malcolm was very close to his stepfather, a very spiritual man and a follower of the Zoroastrian faith. All his life he told Malcolm fables, which he has always remembered — but they didn't mean much to him until a few years ago when his father passed away. Malcolm went to visit the coffin to pay his last respects, only to find the room full of Red Admiral butterflies. The room was enclosed, and no-one could explain how they got in there. Malcolm told others about this, and they saw it for themselves; the insects fluttered above the coffin for the duration of his lying in peace… and then they were gone.

This experience has opened the door for Malcolm on a spiritual level. It was as though his father had to pass away for the spiritual belief to be ignited in him, and for him to continue in his father's footsteps; and also to pass on these tales to his own son, who is already beginning to have a spiritual understanding beyond his years.

Our children are being born into a generation where many of them are much more enlightened than children were even a few decades ago.

Every faith, religion or spiritual belief can be traced back thousands of years. There are so many different views or beliefs that no-one can be completely right. Yet nearly all have a belief in Angels. Everywhere you look, paintings, sculptures and music mention them. It is sheer delight to allow them into our world.

I know, as do many others who have experienced something similar, that Angels, guides and Masters exist. However, explaining the feeling, the warmth of the joy and divine love they bring is very hard. Hopefully you will experience this for yourself one day; it will be extremely personal to you, and that is how it should be. Remember: all you have to do is ask for them to come closer into your life and you may have an unexpected insight, a feeling or a tingle, which is just to let you know they are there.

The meaning of channelling

Channelling with your guides and Angels is done through your psychic third eye and seven centres, known as *chakras*. These are energy points up and down your body which need to be in balance for you to be in harmony with life.

Everyone will have a different experience but I learned early on that you are not normally given more knowledge or experience all at once than you can understand or handle.

When I first discovered this amazing concept and started to experience so much, I wanted to learn *everything*. I couldn't get enough of it. But if I had experienced everything at the beginning I wouldn't have been able to take it all in. My vibrational energy wasn't yet ready; instead it was to be what I call 'drip-fed' into me.

As I raised my vibrational consciousness, my connection became higher and stronger. There have been times when the connection disappears for a while, sometimes for a few months which I find frustrating — but this is normally at times when my energy is low or I have other things going on in my life and 'they' have difficulty getting through to me. It's quite normal.

After I told briefly in my first book the story of my spiritual experiences, I have been taken aback by how many people contacted me from all over the world to say that they have experienced something similar. Many friends whom I had known for years told me they share my beliefs — yet we had never talked about it together! Was this because it's a difficult subject to approach when they are not in the circle of my spiritual friends? I am not sure. Many people want to embrace a more enlightened way of living. Some are doing it, and some never will, however we all need to do it in our own way. There are people like myself doing this, who remain very grounded ... so it doesn't have to be a spaced-out guru way of life!

Because this *is* so personal and individual to everyone seeking a more meaningful existence, it is important to remember never to make another person your Guru, or to follow their every word and believe only their beliefs. Seek out as many ideas as you can, read as much as you can, learn more — and then follow what feels right to you.

Everyone has their own beliefs, different knowledge, and unique experiences. What is right for them may not be right for you. Some are drawn into cults which I personally think can be extremely damaging. Each cult is different so again, like religion, who is right and who is wrong?

A spiritual path is extremely private and personal to you. You alone. It *is* important to share your knowledge, shine your light and encourage others to seek their own enlightenment — but please, never tell people what they should or should not be doing. You can be their guide, their support, give them advice about what you know and feel. However, they will be experiencing something slightly different to what you imagine, and will be feeling it in a different way. This is a gradual process so no-one should be rushed.

I have spoken to and coached many people who have started to experience the beautiful sensation of embracing their guides or Angels in completely different ways. Some are just starting to have spiritual experiences, such as visions or sensations they don't understand, or they feel somehow different by sensing a different energy around them ... every one of them has told me a different story because the experience is individual to them.

It would be interesting to share with you one person's experience because it was so different from mine. I had watched a fascinating video via an Internet site called TED which invites inspiring speakers to talk about their knowledge and experiences. Jill Bolte Taylor, a scientist, talked about an amazing experience when she witnessed her own stroke.

During the experience she felt the atoms *inside* her body connect to the energy *outside* her body. She felt no boundaries and it was as though the inside and outside of her body drifted into one. She felt no physical boundaries and felt light and peaceful; as she drifted in and out of consciousness, she was in what she called 'La La land'.

Jill went on to say that it was as if the air in her body was like a deflated balloon — or that her spirit was so huge that it was as if a genie had come out of its bottle and there was no way she could squeeze this enormous body of hers back into the tiny space of her body. She had found her nirvana. It took her eight years to recover and she has written a fascinating book detailing this experience called *My Stroke of Insight*.

I had thought that just was a one-off until I met J C Mac. A friend, Damien Senn, interviewed J C on his 'People you should meet' live interview website. I listened with great interest as he described what he called *The Anatomy of a Spiritual Meltdown* in which he'd lost his mind through a divine spiritual experience which had changed his life forever.

He had been pursuing a true spiritual understanding for more than twenty-five years and then suddenly, from nowhere, everything changed in an instant. The state was so intense that he couldn't function properly for more than a year, whilst witnessing the absolute beauty of what he now knows as the love of God. He describes his life now as living silently with bliss and a peace beyond anything he could imagine.

This intrigued me so I got in touch with him. J C wanted to share his experiences with others, and agreed to meet me. A few months later, at the 'Power Of Intention' workshop run by Naomi Sassy and

Harun Rabbani, I met Jackie who'd had a very similar experience to JC; I put them in touch.

J C then gave his first talk in London, which of course Jackie and I attended. I was astounded by how many people in the audience had experienced something very similar. There is now a website called 'Spiritual Emergency' in which such people can obtain reassurance that they haven't lost the plot; it also proved to me that everyone has a different and very personal experience.

Something very powerful is happening to thousands of people all over the world. The experiences of J C and Jackie, and of course Malcolm, have been completely different to mine. That is one reason why I say I can never *teach* you this, only demonstrate in my own way.

Spiritual development Circle

This is a group of like-minded people I know, who gather together on a regular basis, to learn and grow their own special connection to the higher powers within the Universe. We each have different spiritual gifts (which we examined in Chapter Five) but each member has some psychic ability which they can develop. Many people know they have a psychic ability in childhood but some choose not to develop it further for various reasons; I am not one of those, I never knew any such thing. I do remember sometimes feeling 'different', but I was never quite sure why.

I have always had what I call my 'inner knowing'. This was so strong, even as a child, that it has given me a lot of confidence — but I never knew where it came from. At times I would simply *know* something and I wouldn't know why; or the words that came out of my own mouth would amaze me and have no connection to what I was thinking. When this happens, it is of course for the benefit of the person I am talking to, rather than myself, and I usually don't remember the words afterwards. This can happen in the middle of an everyday conversation, not just when I am giving spiritual guidance.

I have various guides around me with whom I connect but one I know is a beautiful *Messenger of Light* energy who is a Master. I always know when he is around me because the energy I feel is different and very special because it is lighter. But when we connect to our guides in a Circle, what we do is now called 'channelling'. When you do this, you are connecting to a higher spiritual wisdom through your psychic centres, to receive guidance and helpful information. It is connecting to the Divine Source and all-that-is and opening up to the possibilities that go beyond the conscious mind. To put it in simple terms, we speak telepathically to our guides and guardian angels.

Our Circle meeting usually starts with healing for our friends and family, certain people in need that we know, and around the globe, and for planet Earth. Then we do a group meditation; people's energy connects, which can be much more powerful than meditating alone. Everybody has different energy, and sometimes when the group dynamics change the event can be much more powerful. On occasions we have witnessed some magical moments which have made me feel very humble indeed. It can also change when someone has a much darker energy, making me feel uncomfortable because everyone's energy (including theirs) is strong.

Sometimes we explore a different area. Tarot cards, dowsing, crystals and chakras have been some of the most popular ones. We often do psychometry, where we hold a piece of jewellery from one of the group and tell them what we see and feel, or even hear.

If this is something which may interest you, most areas have Development Circles running. Some people find a Spiritual Church Circle, and attending church, a rich and rewarding experience. The church tends to concentrate more on having mediums passing messages to individuals in the congregation. You don't have to attend any place of worship to be spiritual; it's up to you to find a place to learn and develop your gifts where you feel comfortable. Your own home is as good a place as any.

Meditation, channelling and protection

I have a word to say to those of you reading this who want to take this further: when you start to connect to spirit through deep mediations, it is very important to be sensible and have some guidance. I would not advise you to do this just for the fun of it. There are those who believe you would be wise to put some protection around yourself because you don't want to encourage connecting with unwanted spirits. I don't want to frighten you — but it can happen. People here on Earth are not always nice … so why should they be different once they have passed over? Personally, I believe that most people leave their negative karma behind when they pass over — but there are various different thoughts about this.

There are various beliefs and different styles of meditation, such as Transcendental, Hindu, Buddhist, Shamanism and many others, each practising a different concept. It might be worth your while to look into which practice suits you best before you follow any one of them too far.

I personally have *never* experienced anything nasty, perhaps this is because I don't draw that sort of energy to me. I *know* my guides protect me at all times. To give you another example of why I think this is the case, let me tell you that I have never watched a horror movie in my life. I don't watch violent programmes, thrillers or anything to do with crime. I don't want to experience nightmares or even think about such things, and therefore avoid attracting anything negative or unwanted or that makes me feel uncomfortable into my presence. Some people love to dance with the dark side of spirituality but this can be dangerous. Negative energy attracts negative energy.

Opening up to channel can be a life changing experience but it is usually a gradual process, so don't be frightened. There are various ways to meditate and channel so I will just mention a general non-religious way.

When you start to channel, at the beginning of your meditation ask for your psychic centre to be open; mentally picture your guides and door keepers standing close by. We each have four door keepers who keep us safe; many people like to imagine a coloured cloak around them, which is a form of protection. Visualise this cloak in whatever colour you like — but blue is a good healing colour. Then state your intention, which of course will be for your higher good. When your meditation is over, do remember to ask for your psychic centre to be closed down until you choose for it to be opened again.

If you are ever doing a meditation which feels uncomfortable, stop and ask that spirit to 'go back to the light'. Come out of the meditation and cleanse yourself by gently brushing your body with your hands to clear any negative energy that may still be with you. Rub your hands together first so they become slightly hot, and then gently cleanse the whole of your body from head to toe. Or if you have crystals, dowse them over your body.

Connecting with your guides and Angels is a wonderfully uplifting experience that will help you see the world in a completely different way. It's a skill that can be learned and you do not have to be spiritually evolved or to have been psychic all your life. You *do* need patience, perseverance and a strong desire to make the connection. It gives you a real feeling of peace, that you are not alone, and that our world is made up of love. You begin to feel that love, and you will be able to share yourself with others in a new way because your life will feel more complete.

I highly recommend the book that helped me at the very beginning, which I will mention again. It is called *Opening to Channel* by Sanaya Roman and Duane Packer; there are plenty of other books which may help. Alternatively, seek out someone who belongs to a Circle, with whom you can share your thoughts and experiences, and who can guide you.

I hope you have a wonderful journey when you open your door to a new life — because your life will never be the same. Enjoy it.

Spiritual Orbs

We talked earlier about the energy that surrounds you and that one way to see this is to have an aura photograph taken.

On my first aura photograph that I had taken you can clearly see a large white circle of pure white which I believe is an Orb on my throat. There are many theories as to what a spiritual Orb is — but one thing it is *not* is a trick of light in photography. There is no way that this Orb (which you can see on my website www.sheilasteptoe.com) can be anything other than from spirit or the Angels. Orbs can vary in size and sometimes there maybe more than one in a group photograph.

Angela who took my aura photo said that this Angel Orb was there to tell me that speaking was to be my profession, and that my guides would always be with me helping me with my speech and words. That is why it was on my throat, because that is from where we communicate.

Diana Cooper, who is known as the angel lady because she has made a study of Angels, has on her website many Orb photographs taken all over the world. She has written a book about them too called *Enlightenment through Orbs*. She also mentions that Scientists have verified that Orbs are not lens imperfections or caused by light refracting off particles of dust for instance. In fact, they have concluded that the only possible explanation is that there exists some form of light source within the camera view.

Hypnosis and connecting to your mind

One last thing I would like to add is a quote from Michael Newton's book *Journey of Souls*, which gives a brilliant description of our soul and mind connection:

'How is it possible to reach the soul through hypnosis? Visualise the mind as having three concentric circles, each smaller than the last and within the other, separated only by layers of connected mind-consciousness. The first outer layer is represented by the conscious mind which is our critical, analytic reasoning source. The second layer is the subconscious, where we initially go in hypnosis to tap into the storage area for all the memories that ever happened to us in this life and former lives. The third, the innermost core, is what we are now calling the superconscious mind. This level exposes the highest center of Self where we are an expression of a higher power.

'The superconscious houses our real identity, augmented by the subconscious which contains the memories of the many alter-egos assumed by us in our former human bodies. The superconscious may not be a level at all, but the soul itself. The superconscious mind represents our highest center of wisdom and perspective, and all my information about life after death comes from this source of intelligent energy'.

Let's recap...

STEP 1 — Meditate every day and keep a diary.

STEP 2 — Let go of fears, core conditioning and resistance.

STEP 3 — Practise visualisation and follow your instincts, hunches and sudden ideas.

STEP 4 — Believe in yourself.

STEP 5 — Rise to a challenge. Overcome obstacles and have some fun.

STEP 6 — Your life has a blueprint so let your life unfold as it should be.

STEP 7 — Set your own goals and don't be frightened to step outside your comfort zone.

STEP 8 — We are each part of the same Universe and we each have a reason to be here on Earth.

You need not fear dying because we are all eternal. Your guides and Angels are only a thought away and you can connect to them if we want to — but you need to be open. They cannot reach you through a closed energy field (you).

To put this another way: imagine if you put your hand up to reach something higher than yourself. It's there but just out of your reach. That's how near they are; just a layer of consciousness away.

Follow your own spiritual path, which is unique to you.

Your Angels and Guides

Chapter Nine

You Can Do This Too

I couldn't wait for success: so I went ahead without it.
— *Jonathan Winters, American comedian and actor*

It is hard to believe but as I write this last chapter ... unfortunately, I have to write that part of my own destiny has not happened yet! My distinguished grey-haired man has not yet entered my life. I always said he would be the finale to my book so that I could give hope to others but I still believe and will continue to believe that he will arrive soon.

I am sure it will be such a natural meeting and connection that it will immediately feel right. Right away, I will know he is special to me and worth waiting for. Since my divorce I have had a few deep connections; two of them have a special place in my heart, and have taught me many things. But this one will be different.

Of course, I will have to tell him about all of this gently. It could overwhelm him if I say that I have known about him for years! Can you imagine it? It is possible that we may even grow old disgracefully together, which should be fun. Who knows? I will be content to enjoy the moments day by day and see where this leads. It is exciting though.

He is only part of my destiny, as your destiny includes many aspects of your life. Love, work, relationships, the freedom just to be who you are and to be able to do the things you love in life, are all there. Your destiny will take many years to accomplish as you gradually work towards what you are meant to be doing in this life. Each stage, from your childhood to your senior years, are all gradually building a much bigger picture so each stage is where you should be. What is happening to you is often what is meant to be happening, so you need to learn to work through it with grace rather than with bitterness and hurt. Everything and everybody in your life teaches you something.

But we all have free will. Sometimes we go off-track — but when you go with your flow you will be gradually brought back to the right path as you stop struggling, take your ego out of the equation, and do the things that feel right for you.

Now I want to summarise the ground we have covered in this book. I would also like to share two points of view with you, which in some ways contradict each other, but which I believe to be true.

Do you create your own life by manifesting what you want — or is it pre-planned, as I have discovered that so much of my own life has been? My theory is that you do pre-plan your life with your Masters and guides before you arrive here on Earth. When you create what you want, your subconscious or Higher Self knows what it is that you need to create. *So you do both.*

You live out your life plan and create special events and things, because deep down you know that they are for your own good. They are the bits you create and manifest — but when you go with your flow, it automatically happens, and often better than you could have created yourself.

It can be hard to keep your faith. Many times I have questioned things. You do manifest your life but often things don't happen as you think they will; sometimes what you get is even better than you expect — when you learn to let go of the end result. Often what you want comes along a long time after you have started to want it; the time has to be right. Life is simple — it is you who makes it complicated!

Trusting the Universe and your spiritual helpers will play dividends in the course of your life. Of course you have to put some work in too, and there will always be ups and downs. Yet, difficulties can teach you more and often give you a strength you never knew you had. Learning from them is one of the keys to overcoming them.

Our culture programmes us for success, but do we really understand what success is? Everyone has a different notion as to what success means to them — but we often devote too much time and energy to working and worrying about being successful. Could it be security that we crave, because sometimes it is hard to know when we have arrived as we so often want more? Surely success is about an end to striving and feelings of peace within?

Your attitude is one of the most important aspects of a good life. If you expect life to be good then it will be. If you complain and never see anything good in others and the world around us, then that is what you receive. You get what you expect!

I hope that understanding more about how life works here on Earth will help you realise how much you can achieve. Can you look at life in a different way now, knowing you chose to come here and to work through some of the lessons which are all designed for your spiritual growth?

Think of life as the A-Z of learning. You need to take all the baby steps as you go along the journey of life, eventually to reach a higher level. When you surrender to your flow, life becomes magical. The physical world and the spiritual world can work well together.

You have been here on planet Earth many times before. When you go home, you talk and connect with your soul family, your guides and Masters, about whether to come back again to learn more, or perhaps to stay there for a while. You do still learn in the higher realms but not at such a rapid rate. There are those who believe that you also have the choice to go elsewhere in the Universe to learn something different!

You have the power to choose, moment by moment, who and how you want to be in this world. There is more to life than just *living*. We are all here for a reason and we need to live and learn to our best ability. A feeling deep inside of who you are, as a person, can bring inner peace. Life is not always easy to understand because of some of the experiences that you may go through.

You can create a life which inspires you, and learn to live your true life's path and truths. This might be no more than living a simple life, or you may want to follow a dream. Life is not meant to be a struggle.

All of us are given messages at some time or another. Often you don't listen to them or even realise that they are not just your own thoughts. Do you ever suddenly have inspiration or a sudden flash of vision? I'm talking about those sudden thoughts that make something *click*.

The two most important times when this happens to me are when I am driving and just at the very moment my head is about to hit the pillow! I used to have a pencil and pad by my bed but of course I had to turn the light on to find them, so it is usually easier to get up. I bought myself a Dictaphone which I really should take with me everywhere. I should also take it into my car so that I no longer have the bad habit of writing on a pad on my lap whilst driving! If I don't write these thoughts down when I have them, I forget. I often ask my helpers to remind me later but unfortunately it doesn't always happen like that.

Where is this next stage of my journey going to take me? The ideas keep popping into my head and I have learned to follow them. If I hadn't done that before now, I wouldn't be doing any of this — which has been a huge and magical part of my life.

I have suddenly met so many new people who are opening doors for me to expand my business. Some brilliant new contracts are coming my way. This is exciting. I can't see me ever retiring because I passionately love what I do. It is an honour to have experienced so much wonderful spiritual guidance and I love sharing this with others. That is *why* it happened to me!

Do you follow those hunches and ideas you suddenly have, or do you dismiss them as silly? They are all helpful messages which can show you the right or even the wrong way to proceed. Yet we are all so often worried about the future that we forget to live in the *now*.

You want to control everything and life gets in the way. You make it so. You're so busy running around all the time, trying to do everything and keeping up with the rat-race, that you forget to concentrate on yourself. You are important — *everyone* is — but if you can learn to live in a much simpler way (and I don't mean to be financially poor or suffering) then you can journey down the river of life, swimming with the tide. The struggles which so often take you over will gradually subside.

Magical things become a magnet as you begin to draw them into your life, when you learn to let go.

There are many universal spiritual laws to live by, which can help with your flow. I will mention a few that you may like to incorporate into your own life — but there are many others which you might like to look up later:

- **The Law of Manifestation**

You become what you think about the most. So, as the old adage goes, *Be careful what you wish for — you will probably get it.*

- **The Law of Duality**

There is a flipside or opposite to everything. You can only know good if there is evil. Light can only exist with dark. To experience success you must know failure.

- **The Law of Cycles**

Everything and all events occur in cycles. Things will be good for a while and then suddenly — *boom!* — everything crashes. You must make the most of the good times, keep your head above water in the bad times, and wait for the next reversal.

- **The Law of Evolution**

Everything evolves and changes. Nothing stands still forever so ensure you progress and move ahead.

- **The Law of Choices**

You have control over the choices you make. You have the power to control your destiny and your possibilities are unlimited. Stop feeling trapped; stop being a victim of your circumstances.

- **The Law of Responsibility**

You must accept the outcome of the choices you make.

- **The Law of Synchronicity**

We are each part of the Universe, not a separate entity. Your actions affect those around you and determine how your life is shaped. When you see the connection to the world around you, you understand the control you have over your destiny.

- **The Law of Attraction**

Energy attracts. You attract everything into your life, both positive and negative things, and events.

- **The Law of Intention**

What you intend is powerful and will manifest.

- **The Law of Cause and Effect**

This is also known as **The Law of Karma**. It means that you get out of life what you put into it. You reap what you sow.

- **The Law of Compassion and The Law of Consideration**

These are two separate laws which speak for themselves. 'Do unto others as you would have them do unto you.'

- **The Law of Faith**

Believe in the fulfilment of your desires, and they will be fulfilled.

- **The Law of Forgiveness**

Prophets and spiritual teachers throughout the ages have taught us that to forgive ourselves and our fellow man is one of the greatest gifts you can learn.

- **The Law of Mental Imaging**

One of the most exciting things you can master is visualisation. The mind has magical powers. It creates the pictures and plans which you turn into reality.

- **The Law of Healing**

Everyone has healing energy, an electromagnetic field that lies within and around the body. You can mentally send this healing to your own body and to others.

- **The Law of Praise**

Praise the negative as well as the positive experiences and don't forget to say thank you when you receive them.

- **Law of Detachment**

The wisdom of uncertainty leads to freedom.

- **Law of Giving and Receiving**

Give to others and learn to receive yourself.

One of the most important things I have learned is that the physical world and the spiritual world are a world of our own self-evolution. You can work together so beautifully. Embracing your spiritual helpers adds an extra dimension, one where there are no limits.

You need to make the most of your life and enjoy all that you can. You have to understand that you are in control of your own life.

But … and there is a big 'but' here … nothing will change in your life unless you make it happen. Wanting and talking about it is a very different thing to actually *achieving* something. You need to know what you want, take action and put *energy* into it, to make it become reality!

There are four different energy bodies: physical, mental, emotional and spiritual. Raising the energy of one will have an effect on the others. When all four are in alignment, your energy will be very high and very powerful. You will be able to create whatever you want to in life.

The most important things to create your own success and get the most from your life are these important steps:

STEP 1 — Meditate every day and keep a diary.

STEP 2 — Let go of fears, core conditioning and resistance.

STEP 3 — Practise visualisation and follow your instincts, hunches and sudden ideas.

STEP 4 — Believe in yourself.

STEP 5 — Rise to a challenge. Overcome obstacles and have some fun.

STEP 6 — Your life has a blueprint so let your life unfold as it should be.

STEP 7 — Set your own goals and don't be frightened to step outside your comfort zone.

STEP 8 — You need not fear dying because we are all eternal.

STEP 9 —

- **Meditate**: Fifteen minutes a day is the best 'me' time you can give yourself because you reap so much benefit. As you progress, you can build up to longer.

- **Visualise**: What you visualise you materialise. Imagination is everything.
- **Affirmations**: These are powerful words that work magic.
- **Set your goals**: You need to be clear and precise but realistic, focused on the end result.
- **Your thoughts** create your reality. You can't afford to send mixed messages to the Universe!
- **Small steps are believable** and therefore achievable. They lead to the top of the ladder.
- **Follow your** feelings, emotions and gut instincts — they tell you so much.
- **Listen** to the voices and whispers in your head — your messages are planted here!
- **Ask for guidance** from your Higher Self, spiritual guides and Angels. They are waiting but you have to ask.
- **Your spiritual path is personal and unique to yourself**: You can learn from others but you must walk your own truth.
- **You mustn't get cross** if 'life' gets in the way sometimes. If you keep trying you will succeed.
- **Relax.** Life doesn't have to be so stressful so go with your flow.
- **The most important thing to remember is**: You are perfect just as you are right now. You are exactly where you are meant to be in this journey of life.
- **Let go of the past and live in the now**: You shouldn't worry about the future — just know that with your positive attitude it will be wonderful.

I have loved writing this book. I hope it has helped you understand a little more about how the universal energy and you can work together to make your life as magical as it can be. Remember, you are never alone; all you need to do is ask for extra guidance and support. They are waiting!

The guidance you will receive, the sensations you will feel and the inner serenity you suddenly experience are better than winning a million on the Lottery. It is a divine love which is surrounding you all right now, all over the world, and I wish that I could rub a lamp and produce a genie for you to feel this, and for you to know that it is there just waiting to come into your life right now. Unfortunately I can't rub or perform that sort of magic for you — but *you* can.

Please be patient: it doesn't always happen in an instant. It is often a gradual process but one worth striving for. Sometimes you need to take small steps at first rather than trying to climb to the top in one. There is no rush.... but to feel the peace and serenity inside will be worth everything.

So. What are you going to do with your life now? The latest item on *my* agenda was learning to fly an aeroplane on my sixtieth birthday, not too long ago! The sky's the limit and I fully intended to be up there — literally.

Do you fancy flying in the sky too? I would love to meet as many of you as I can during my presentation talks. Or, if you would like to attend one of my workshops, then it would be my pleasure to take you on to the next stage of your journey.

To put in a nutshell how I feel now, and how I hope you can feel too, here is a quote from a channelled book by a Master of light called Orin, a spiritual guide and teacher from the higher realms, called *Spiritual Growth — Being your Higher Self*, by Sanaya Roman:

'Spiritual growth is similar to personal growth, with one big difference: when you grow spiritually you are connecting with a higher power and using that connection to empower your growth. This higher power — your Higher Self and God/All-That-Is — works with your personality self, assisting it to develop self-confidence, self-love, clarity, and other important qualities. When you work on your personal growth and add to that your connection to a higher power, your journey is even more joyful, rapid, and transformative.'

Enjoy the rest of your journey!

I Made it Happen

Flying High

Would you like to explore a little more?

Appendix A

Ideas For Further Reading

Acupuncture — Ancient Chinese medicine technique of inserting and manipulating fine fuliform needles into specific meridian parts of the body to heal and restore natural balance

Alexander Technique — body re-education and coordination which is accomplished through physical and psychological principles

Aloha or **Huna** — Hawaiian spiritual teachings

Aloe Vera — natural products for health taken from the sap of the plant. Used for anti-inflamatory, anti-bacterial, anti-viral and energy tonic purposes

Angels — a spiritual supernatural being found in many religions, and known as Messengers from God

Aromatherapy — the use of essential oils

Astrology Reading — birth chart analysis to know 'self' depending on where the planets here are the time, date and place of your birth

Aura — the electromagnetic energy field surrounding your body, varying in colours depending on the state of your health

Aura Photography — special Kirlian photography to capture your aura on a photograph

Chakras — seven energy centres aligned down your body

Chiropractor — a professional therapist who performs alignment of spine and surrounding muscles

Counselling — normally a one-to-one session with a trained counsellor, although group sessions are also common where you share the counsellor with other clients in a session

Cranio-Sacral Therapy — hands-on non-invasive healing to help the body self-repair. Suitable for all ages including babies as it is so gentle

Crop Circles — man made or are they from outer space? The debate is ongoing!

Crystal Balls — crystal or glass ball believed to aid clairvoyants to predict the future

Crystals — a mineral formed in nature whose energy can be used for healing

Dowsing — divination using an object to search for something else. It is also possible to dowse using a crystal over an object

Emotional Freedom Technique (EFT) — tapping certain meridian points in the body to release negative energy

Feng Shui — ancient Chinese tradition for balancing your environment

Flower Remedies — variety of natural remedies for healing

Healing and Healers — people who perform complementary and alternative ways of healing using the hands

Herbal medicine — a traditional and folk medicine practice using plant and plant extracts

Homeopathic medicine — popular alternative medicine treating the whole person using safe natural remedies

Hopi Ear — candle treatment inserted in ears for clearing the sinuses

Hypnosis/Hypnotherapy — accessing the subconscious mind and thoughts, to manage emotional problems and addictions, by a fully trained therapist

Indian Head Massage — scalp, neck and face massage to clear and open your energy channels

Iridology — diagnostic tool which looks into your eyes to reveal the state of your body health

Kinesiology — body-balancing by applying the sciences of biomechanics, anatomy, physiology and motor learning

Life Coaching — motivational support and guidance with a trained coach, normally to ease a personal or career transition

Magnetic Therapy — application to the magnetic field, of electromagnetic devices or permanent static magnets, to the body for health benefits. Often bracelets or jewellery are worn

Meditation — quieting of the mind into a deeper state of relaxation

Medicine or **Animal Cards** — based on ancient Native American wisdom, through healing with the power of certain animals

Mediums — individuals who channel communication with spirits

Metaphysics — investigates principles of reality transcending science, including cosmology and ontology, to try to explain the world

Mind Mapping — a useful planning tool, which is a diagram used to represent words, ideas, tasks and other items linked to a project or problem

Native American 'Indians' — indigenous people of the Americas, far back in history

Neuro-Linguistic Programming (NLP) — a method applied to interpersonal communicating and psychotherapy

Numerology — what your name and birth date reveal about your life path, destiny

Ouija Board — a flat board with letters and numbers used to communicate with Spirit

Osteopath — a trained person who uses manipulation of your bones or muscles to ease discomfort or pain, usually after an injury

Paganism — an ancient pre-Christ religion still practised today

Palmistry — reading of your hands and fingers, which has been an interest for humans since the Stone Age

Past Life Regression — a technique that uses hypnosis to recall past lives

Pilates — subtle exercise focusing on the core postural muscles to keep the body balanced

Psychology — an academic and applied science involving the study of mental functions and behaviour

Psychic surgery — the use of paranormal means to conduct an alleged invasive medical procedure using the practitioner's bare hands

Psychometry — the ability to relate details about the past or future condition of an object, person or location. Often a psychic reading can be demonstrated through holding one of a person's possessions

Quantum Physics — a branch of physics dealing with the behaviour of matter and energy on the minute scale of atoms and subatomic particles. The Quantum arena is fundamental to our understanding of all of the forces of nature except gravity

Reflexology — gentle manipulation of various part of the body such as feet, hands and ears, which correspond with organs in the zones of the body, for general good health

Reiki — holistic healing, seeking to bring people to a state of wholeness in body, mind and spirit

Remote Viewing — the attempt to gather information about a distant or unseen target using paranormal means or extra-sensory perception

Rune Stones — typically a stone with a raised runic coloured inscription; many can be traced back to the later Viking age. Nowadays, rune stones are used for divination

Séance — an attempt to communicate with Spirit, often using a Ouija Board (see above)

Shamanism — an ancient spiritual practice concerned with communicating with the spirit and animal world, and still practised today throughout the world

Shiatsu — Japanese massage using the body's energy system

Tai Chi — a gentle Chinese martial art, often practised for health and longevity reasons

Tarot Cards — 78 cards, often used in fortune telling

Telepathy — sensing the thoughts of others

Trance Channelling — allowing Spirit to speak through you

Visualisation — creating mental imagery

Witches and **Witchcraft** — the use of certain kinds of supernatural or magical powers; an ancient tradition still practised in many countries. There are black and white witches, usually engaging in the casting of spells

Yoga — a combination of breathing exercises, physical posture and meditation which has been practised for more than 5,000 years. There are over 100 different variations

Zoroastrianism —very old eastern religion/faith

Appendix B

Places To Visit Or Read About

Ancient monuments, sacred places, and spiritual sites worldwide. To discover these, I recommend the following websites:
www.sacred-destinations.com and www.sacredsites.com

Websites exist covering every subject listed above, and more. For more advanced information I suggest a visit to
www.crystalinks.com and www.crystallotus.com

Libraries and the Mind Body Spirit section of your local bookshop are a good source of information.

Angel Forums — It can be fun to write to your Angels and guides to let them know what you truly want. Of course you can speak to them in your mind, as we have discussed, but sometimes writing it down seals the beliefs.

On a piece of paper I draw one big circle in the middle, with lots of bubbles or clouds scattered about in each corner, and in each section I write a request. I try to group relationships, work, or problem areas together so that clusters form on the single page. I also write which Angels I would like to draw closer to me for the next six months — because different Angels can help with special areas. This is sometimes called an Angel Conference.

Messengers of Light by Terry Lynn Taylor is a book explaining about the different Angels and what they mean. There are many variations that I have not mentioned including Cheerleaders, Muses, Copilots and Fairies, and you can draw them into your life for different reasons. For example, call in the Mirth Makers when you are having a party, the Prosperity Brokers for wealth and of course Cupid for love.

Sheila Steptoe

I then fold this piece of paper and put it somewhere special; or sometimes I burn it and release my wishes to the Universe.

Appendix C

Further Thinking And Tips

You have read my story, and what many people believe about how it all works. Do you feel ready to take your first steps on your own spiritual journey? Here are some simple useful tips or work sheets which you can copy and complete.

Simple actions:

Write down your goal. Make it realistic.

_____
_____
_____
_____

Write down WHY you want to achieve it.

_____
_____
_____
_____

Make a list of things you need to do:

Action 1_____
Action 2_____
Action 3_____
and so on...

What spare time commitment can you give to this?
_____
_____
_____
_____

What financial commitment?
_____
_____

Timescale _____

Your commitment and the steps you need to take:
Write down:

Each day…………………......What I did

Each week…………….....… What I achieved

Each month……….…..……What I will do/have done

1 month…………….…....…How far have I come?

3 months……….…….……..Getting there

Positives…………….…......Negatives…………………….......

Mishaps/delays……….…......Achieving balance……………......

Now take a look at the structure of your day: what is good about it?

What could you change to make it even better?

What time are you wasting each day?

Priorities — Before   Now

First thing............................   ....

Morning...............................   ....

Mid morning.........................   ....

Lunchtime...........................   ....

Mid afternoon.......................   ....

Early evening........................   ....

Evening..............................   ....

Weekends............................   ....

Good day....................Why   Bad day............Why

What works well...
_____
_____

Most impact...
_____
_____

How do you feel now?
_____
_____

What do you need to work on?
_____
_____

What could you get rid of?
_____
_____

What looks like being your next opportunity?
_____
_____

What challenges (not problems!) am I facing now?
_____
_____

What is my achievable time frame for meeting them?
_____
_____

I will...
_____
_____

Appendix D

Books, People And Websites

Chapter One

Conversations with God
by Neale Donald Walsch
Hampton Roads Publishing Company ISBN 978-1571740564

Opening to Channel
by Duane Packer and Sanaya Roman
H J Kramer ISBN 978-0915811052

James Arthur Ray (quotation) www.harmonicwealth.com

Unexpected Miracles: The Gift of Synchronicity and How to Open It
by David Richo, PhD
Crossroads Publishing Co ISBN 978-0824517298

The Secret
by Rhonda Byrne
Atria Books/Beyond Words ISBN 978-1582701707
— film at www.thesecret.tv

What The Bleep Do We Know
— film at www.whatthebleepdoweknow.com

The Opus
— film at www.theopus.net

Mindlab™ USA
— light and sound machine. There are various places to purchase it on the Internet including www.mindmodulations.com/products.html

Chapter Two

Randy Gage
— Yes Group 25th April 2007 www.yesgroup.org and www.randygage.com

The Shift
— film at www.theshiftmovie.com

Princes Trust www.princes-trust.org.uk

College of Psychic Studies, London www.collegeofphysicstudies.co.uk

Mindy Gibbins-Klein www.thebookmidwife.co.uk

The Work We Were Born to Do
by Nick Williams
Element Books ISBN 978-1862045521

Chapter Three

Mind Body Soul exhibition
— run by www.primeimpact.co.uk

Ask and It Is Given
by Esther & Gerry Hicks
Hay House ISBN 978-1401904593

Living Magically
by Gill Edwards
Piatkus Books ISBN 978-0749917432

A New Earth: Awaken to your True Life's Purpose
by Eckhart Tolle
Gale Cengage ISBN 978-1577316510

The Power of Intention
by Dr Wayne W Dyer
Hay House ISBN 978-1401902155

The Intention Experiment
by Lynne McTaggart

Free Press ISBN 978-0743276955

Loving What Is
by Byron Katie www.thework.com
Harmony ISBN 978-0609608746

The Institute of HeartMath Research Centre (USA)
www.heartmath.org

Alternatives www.alternatives.org.uk
St James Church, Piccadilly, London W1J 9LL

The Sedona Method www.sedonamethod.com

Ecademy: professional business networking
www.ecademy.com

Professional Speakers Association
www.professionalspeakersassociation.co.uk or www.nsaspeakers.org

Lesley Morrissey www.insidenews.co.uk

Chapter Four

A Return to Love
by Marianne Williamson
Harper Paperbacks ISBN 978-0060927486

Feel the Fear and Do It Anyway
by Susan Jeffers
Ballantyne Books ISBN 978-0449902929

Healthy Life — Mind Body and Soul magazine
www.healthylifeessex.co.uk/the_magazine.html

Arthur Findlay College www.arthurfindlaycollege.org
Stansted Hall, Stanstead, Essex CM24 8UD

Toastmasters www.toastmasters.org or www.natuk.com

Business Link
— To find your local office visit www.businesslink.gov.uk

Chapter Five

You Can Heal Your Life
by Louise Hay
Hay House ISBN 978-0937611012

Jonny Kennedy: The Boy Whose Skin Fell Off
— DebRa is the charity for people with Dystrophic Epidermolysis Bullsa (EB) www.debra.org.uk
— www.channel4.com/fourdocs/archive/boy_whose_skin.html

Chapter Six

Nick Williams & Niki Hignett www.inspired-entrepreneur.com

Chapter Seven

Grandparents Association www.grandparent-association.org.uk

Moot House
The Stow, Harlow, Essex CM20 3AG

Alan Stevens, Media Coach www.mediacoach.co.uk

Chapter Eight

Chalice Well Gardens www.chalicewell.org.uk
Chilkwell Street, Glastonbury, Somerset BA6 8DD

My Stroke of Insight
Jill Bolte Taylor Ph.D
Lulu.com ISBN 978-1430300618
TED films www.ted.com/index.php/talks/jill_bolte_taylor

Enlightenment Through Orbs
by Diana Cooper and Kathy Crosswell
C&C Publishing ISBN 978-0955908309

J C Mac www.jcmac.net

Damien Senn www.peopleyoushouldmeet.com

Diana Cooper
Author of books about Angels www.dianacooper.com

Journey of Souls: Case Studies of Life Between Lives
by Michael Newton
Llewellyn Publications ISBN 978-1567184853

Many Lives, Many Masters
by Brian Weiss
Fireside ISBN 978-0671657864

Support in a spiritual emergency www.spiritualcrisisnetwork.org.uk

Chapter Nine

A Little Light on the Spiritual Laws
by Diana Cooper
Mobius ISBN 978-0340768631

Spiritual Growth: Being Your Higher Self
by Sanaya Roman
H J Kramer ISBN 978-0915811120

Appendix B

Messengers of Light
by Terry Lynn Taylor
H J Kramer ISBN 978-0915811519

Appendix E

School For Parents, College For Carers

This material is borrowed from my first book, in case you haven't read it yet. Bringing up children is an important role for anyone. Your children's lives can be influenced so easily, which is why I have included this here.

You only learn about parenting from your own upbringing, and we all make mistakes. Sometimes it would be good to explain this to our children! Here is what you should aim for:

- We can admire our children. We can tell them how much we love them and how clever they are.
- We can tell them how proud we are of them.
- We can encourage them to discuss and share their feelings.
- We can encourage our children by supporting them in a positive way.
- We can praise our children — but also point out that they learn from their own mistakes.
- We should encourage them to be honest with themselves and truthful to others.
- We can encourage them not to feel a failure if they are not top of the class, by pointing out other qualities they possess.
- We can help our children to develop respect for themselves, and for others.
- We can learn that if we shout at them — they may shout back.
- We can learn that if we swear at them — they will swear back.
- We can learn to be a good example to them as they learn from us.

- We can learn that quality time with each other is precious.
- We can learn that a hug can sometimes be enough and says more than words ever can.
- We can learn that our children have their own dreams and must follow their own path.
- We can help them build on their self-esteem.

Questionnaire for kids

- What makes you cross within the family?
  (Parents? siblings? something else?)
- How could we change this pattern? What would you like to see us do differently?
- Do you feel you can come to me at any time and talk to me?
- Shall we set some time aside every day — just the two of us?
- When would be the best time for both of us?
- Would you like more help with your homework?
- Can we talk HONESTLY with each other?
- Could you help me more?
- How do you feel about school or college? Do you like *all* your friends?
- If I had to tell you off, what do you think would be a fair punishment?
- Would you like to go on an outing as a family more often?
- If so, where would you like to go?
  (For a meal/museum/shopping/park/swimming/cinema/bowling/something else?)
- Would it be nice for us all to have our meals together every night so we could then talk about our day?
- If I helped you more, would you help me more?

- What incentive would you like to help you do better? What reward could I give you?
- If you do well in something, how would you like to be praised?
- How do you feel about me as a parent? Have I supported you in the best way I can?

Adults vs children

If we respect them — they will respect us.

If we listen to them — they will listen to us.

If we hear them — they will hear us too.

If we shout at them — they will shout back.

If we swear at them — they will swear back.

If you tell them they *can't* — they will believe that and rebel.

If we 'think' for them — they will grow up confused.

Lightning Source UK Ltd.
Milton Keynes UK
UKHW041917090419
340750UK00001B/70/P